Inferiority Complex

A Short Guide to Overcoming Inferiority Complex

(The Ultimate Guide to Raise Your Self-esteem and Overcome Your Inferiority Complex)

Richard Binns

Published By **Simon Dough**

Richard Binns

All Rights Reserved

Inferiority Complex: A Short Guide to Overcoming Inferiority Complex (The Ultimate Guide to Raise Your Self-esteem and Overcome Your Inferiority Complex)

ISBN 978-1-998901-68-5

No part of this guidbook shall be reproduced in any form without permission in writing from the publisher except in the case of brief quotations embodied in critical articles or reviews.

Legal & Disclaimer

The information contained in this book is not designed to replace or take the place of any form of medicine or professional medical advice. The information in this book has been provided for educational & entertainment purposes only.

The information contained in this book has been compiled from sources deemed reliable, and it is accurate to the best of the Author's knowledge; however, the Author cannot guarantee its accuracy and validity and cannot be held liable for any errors or omissions. Changes are periodically made to this book. You must consult your doctor or get professional medical advice before using any of the suggested remedies, techniques, or information in this book.

Upon using the information contained in this book, you agree to hold harmless the Author from and against any damages, costs, and expenses, including any legal fees potentially resulting from the application of any of the information provided by this guide. This disclaimer applies to any damages or injury caused by the use and application, whether directly or indirectly, of any advice or information presented, whether for breach of contract, tort, negligence, personal injury, criminal intent, or under any other cause of action.

You agree to accept all risks of using the information presented inside this book. You need to consult a professional medical practitioner in order to ensure you are both able and healthy enough to participate in this program.

Table of Contents

Chapter 1: What Is An Inferiority Complex? 1

Chapter 2: Feeling Inferior 6

Chapter 3: Inferiority Complex 16

Chapter 4: How To Overcome Inferiority Complex? 21

Chapter 5: Peer Pressure 39

Chapter 6: Understanding Inferiority 44

Chapter 7: Root Causes of Inferiority Complex 55

Chapter 8: Prevention Is Better Than Cure 65

Chapter 9: Climbing The Ladder 80

Chapter 10: A Step in Building Your Self Confidence 89

Chapter 11: A Philosophy to Increase Your Self Confidence 93

Chapter 12: Building Confidence and Self Esteem 97

Chapter 13: The Roots of Low Self Confidence 101

Chapter 14: Thoughts on Improving Self Confidence 105

Chapter 15: What to Do When You Need to Boost Your Self Confidence 109

Chapter 16: Advises to Help You in Increasing Self Confidence 113

Chapter 17: Build Self-confidence from Within 117

Chapter 1: What Is An Inferiority Complex?

Inadequacy and feelings of inferiority are all part of the inferiority complex. The feelings can arise because of an physical flaw or due to circumstances in which we feel that we're less intelligent than our colleagues. In other situations it could be the result of completely imaginary flaws.

Feeling inadequate extends to more than disappointment over a colleague's promotion or sadness over a poor grade on a broader class exam. These are normal, perhaps healthy reactions to disappointments and generally nothing to worry about.

But, it's not rare for people who has this disorder to appear introverted in faces of people who make them feel inadequate. In other instances, one may attempt to cover up any perceived flaw they may are experiencing by acting in an exce... competitive way. They could also beha... violently toward others in certain situations.

The Meaning of the Term 'Complex of Inferiority'

A feeling of inferiority is described in the American Psychological Association (APA) as "a basic feeling of inadequacy and insecurity, arising from genuine or imagined physical or psychological insufficiency." (1) The term was coined by renowned psychologist Alfred Adler in 1907 to explain the reasons why many people do not have the desire to act in their best interests and to pursue their dreams in life. Today, psychiatrists, psychologists and other professionals in the field of mental health do not use the word and instead refer to it as low self-esteem as Maddux mentions.

Inferiority Complex Signs and Symptoms

Martin E. Ford, PhD, professor and deputy dean in George Mason University's College of Education and Human Development located in Fairfax, Virginia, states, "Feeling inadequate from time to time is human nature." "How one reacts to those feelings is crucial. Do they inspire you to learn and strive for greater success? Do they make you ruminate and shut down, or do they make you ruminate and shut down? Do they make you envious of others and make you put people down in order to build yourself up? Or, even worse, do they make you jealous of others and make you put people down in order to build yourself up? Or do you want to always place blame on others for problems for which you should take responsibility? The term 'inferiority complex' may be applied when such patterns become constant over a wide range of contexts."

You've likely felt self-doubt and anxiety at times throughout your life. But, if your self-image is negative throughout your day there's a chance you're suffering from an inner demon.

The disorder, first identified as early as 1907 by the psychologist Alfred Adler, is characterized by specific symptoms of the mind that make it difficult to perform daily tasks.

It is still recognized as a possible cause of suffering, even though it's not considered to be a "disease" in modern psychiatry. It is possible that the feelings of feeling inadequate compared to others could be real or imaginary. According to research that was published on September 14, 2014, in The North American Journal of Medical Sciences If they are not addressed they may develop into deeper feelings of inadequate and lead to a myriad of other symptoms.

Symptoms That Are Most Common

Complex symptoms of inferiority are more than an occasional feeling of self-esteem loss or doubts about your capabilities and abilities; they're chronic. Refrain from regular social activities and situations Comparing yourself to others Insanity, irritability or violence inability to complete tasks The signs are of anxiety, depression, or other mental health issues.

People with an inferiority disorder may appear narcissistic or confident sometimes, but it's not always the scenario. In reality, it's a way to conceal a soaring feeling of inadequateness. Overly competitive Being an person who is a perfectionist, or sensitive to critique Finding flaws in others Needing attention accepting mistakes are just a few indicators.

People with an inferiority disorder are likely have experienced childhood events that can trigger their symptoms. A single incident is seldom enough to trigger an ongoing condition.

Chapter 2: Feeling Inferior
: A Guide to Your Emotions

If we feel unworthy most of the time, it's due to the fact that we compare ourselves with others and think we're not up to par. Let's face it that it happens often. It's possible to be scrolling through your Instagram feed and see a new image from someone who you are following. You you think, "Wow, how can you not be amazed by how perfect they are? ?!?" I'm not going to appear as perfect no regardless of the filters I employ! Maybe you're invited to an event only to discover that you're in a space packed with accomplished people who have interesting lives. The idea of speaking to them causes you to be nervous. Then, you're gazing at the door and contemplating the best strategy to get out. You might be visiting your spouse's family members for the first time, and you are worried that you might not be accepted or that they'll judge you as not worthy. You might be easily scared by other people and worry about the opinions of others about you even though you are not in control of it. Being judged as inferior can cause major mental turmoil. It affects our self-esteem and causes us to be skeptical of our talents. In addition, it is possible that it could cause us to feel lonely. However, that's not the case, and we're here to tell you! There's no reason to feel insecure from time-to-time We're here to help you get through the feeling.

A Deeper Look at Feeling Inferior

What is it to feel inferiority? Dictionary.com provides a couple of definitions to help you. "adj. less significant, valuable, or worthy" is the one that gets closest to feeling less important, valuable, or worthy. Don't you think they hit the nail right on the head?

Due to a myriad of reasons it is possible to feel inadequate. Perhaps a colleague receives the promotion you've always wanted, and then you start to doubt your own skills and abilities. This can make you think that you aren't sufficient when someone has a breakup with you. You might compare yourself to an older sibling who appears to be the recipient of all the praise from your parents which makes you feel that your achievements aren't as important. Do we feel that we're less worthy or is this something we believe to justify being unable to meet our own standard?

There's no doubt that you've heard of superiority complexes in which people feel that they're superior to other people. Did you know that there's also an underlying feeling of being inadequate? This is true! When we experience low self-esteem over a long period of period of time, we may develop an insecurity that leads us to believe that all the negative self-talk and self-doubt are totally justifiable. This type of mental illness causes you to judge yourself and ponder every flaw even when you're at your lowest. It's not a great thing to be a part of!

If we are feeling inferior and feel inadequate, we can be prone to a condition known as self-fulfilling prophesy. You are self-critical that you are prone to failing and this only increases your discontent. It becomes difficult task to break the vicious cycle!

"No one can make you feel inferior without your agreement," Eleanor Roosevelt reportedly declared. To help you shift your perspective, keep in mind this phrase whenever you feel inadequate. Nobody else can take over this situation except you! Aren't you impressed?

How Feeling Inferior Shows Up Mentally

A feeling of being unworthy could affect your mental well-being. Here are some signs that you may notice as you experience this feeling:

Self-esteem is low.

Feeling uncomfortable, uncomplete or not worthy

- Comparing oneself with other people

Easily angry anger, impatient, or angry

- Nature of competition

A difficult time accepting errors or failures

• Sensitivity to criticism, and perfectionists

This feeling can fluctuate and change. We often experience every now and then particularly when we're meeting strangers or are in some unusual situation. The feeling usually fades when we are more relaxed or begin to manage our feelings of feeling inadequate. However, if you're experiencing difficulty coping with these emotions on by yourself, seeking help from a mental health professional is a great idea! We don't want those unpleasant emotions to hinder you or have a lasting effect on your quality of life.

How Feeling Inferior Shows Up Physically

The feeling of being unworthy can manifest as physical symptoms the same way that it affects your mental well-being. Here are a few scenarios of how you could experience:

Social withdrawal

- Inability to complete tasks

- Sleeping problems/insomnia

Being apathetic can make us feel more isolated, which can make us feel further. It is possible that we have trouble with our daily activities however, we are not likely to seek help from anyone else. Stress and emotional stress can affect our immune systems, create chest pain, and lead to muscles to tighten. These signs could be an indication of depression, anxiety or other mental health problems in the event that they persist and become difficult to control. If you feel that your life is affected, we suggest seeking help by a specialist in mental health.

5 Methods in order to Cope with Feeling inferior

Do not worry! There are coping strategies that can help you in dealing with your feelings. Try them for yourself and let us know what you think!

1. Speak to yourself with compassion.

We are prone to make ourselves feel inferior and then be very harsh with ourselves when we feel like we aren't good enough. Do not make the mistake of becoming your own worst critic! Instead, build your self-confidence and self-esteem by telling yourself positive things that make you feel good You might be in a bad mood But I'm aware of the value I have. My qualifications, possessions or appearance don't determine my worthiness. I have everything I need.

2. Get help or make contact with a friend.

I can get by with the help of my friends according to the Beatles song suggests! Contact someone whom you can count on and will be there to help you. It's possible that you feel unworthy in the moment however it doesn't mean that you have to be on your own! Let all your negative feelings from your mind. A person who can affirm our feelings is extremely helpful!

3. Do yourself a favor by giving yourself a pep talk and make use of a motivating word.

Comparing ourselves to others reduces our self-esteem and makes us feel unimportant. To turn negative thoughts around, it's sometimes necessary for ourselves to be handed a jog talk. I'm not in the best mood this moment however, I'll make it through it! It's not the only time that I've experienced this and it's not the last time. It will all be fine!

4. Be as careful of yourself as though you were your friend.

It's okay if you don't have someone available to help you now. You're able to help yourself! Imagine how you would want someone to comfort you in this circumstance. Do yourself a favor or eat some junk food or relax on the sofa with a cuddly, warm blanket, and watch your preferred Netflix show. You can be the person you're searching for now!

5. Keep a journal

It's not like homework. Note down what you're thinking, including deep and dark thoughts you're not willing to think about. You'll be able to change the perspective and challenge negative thoughts with greater clarity by doing this. Create a list of everything you love about yourself or that distinguishes you from other people (in the best way). Be sure to trust us when we say you'll likely fill the pages.

It's that simple. it. We hope this helps to overcome the feeling of being inadequate while reminding you you're not by yourself! We already think that you're pretty amazing.

Chapter 3: Inferiority Complex

The Tendency to Blame Others

Someone who suffers from an inferiority disorder often blames others for their struggles and blames their weaknesses on the causes that are that are beyond their control, like their childhood. As per the Depression Alliance, most of these behaviors are used as a way for people to redress their negative perceptions of themselves.

The Signs of Being Inferior. Feeling Inferior

Feeling inferior and feeling like you're inferior are two different things. You may be able to see that someone is more taller than you for instance. Perhaps you don't have the physique of an elite athlete. These are all valid and valid observations.

But the fact that you realize you're not as good as someone else in a particular way doesn't mean that you must be a victim of this. Feeling inadequate can result in intrusive thoughts which may indicate that you have an inferiority disorder.

Two Types of Inferiority Complex

Adler identified two kinds of inferiority complexes.

Primary Inferiority may start in the early years of childhood because of feeling insecure and being unfairly judged by the other. As an adult, it could result in an inferiority disorder.

Secondary Inferiority is when people do not achieve their own self-perceived success and security goals. In the end as per GoodTherapy.com those who have lingering feelings of inadequacy from childhood could become worse.

Complexes of Inferiority. Superiority

While superiority complex and inferiority complex are considered to be opposite diseases They often coincide and are often co-existent.

Superiority is the belief that you are superior to other people in particular ways. They might exaggerate their achievements and achievements to exaggerate about their accomplishments. While these behavior patterns may appear as if they are incompatible with someone suffering from an inferiority disorder, according to the Adler psychological theory, a person who appears to be superior is usually hiding the feelings of helplessness, weakness and dependence.

"The superiority complex is one of the methods that a person with an inferiority... complex may employ as a strategy of escape from his challenges," according to the writings of Adler. The person believes that he is superior even though he's in reality, while his illusion of success compensates his inability to accept his shortcomings. The average person does not possess a superiority complex and does not think he is superior. He strives to be more superior just as we all strive to achieve success; however so long as the aspire is manifested at work, it does not cause false perceptions that are the basis of mental disease.

Recognizing a person with inferiority or Superiority Complex

It's not easy to recognize those who display an attitude of superiority, or inequality disorder because their behavior doesn't necessarily reflect their true thoughts and beliefs.

They could attempt at making you feel unsecure For instance, they may try to make you feel uneasy.

They're always seeking approval from other people.

They constantly boast about their achievements.

There are lots of complaints.

They exhibit an over sensibility to criticism.

They constantly criticize other people.

They experience mood swings frequently.

They are more likely to stay away from social situations.

They are having a difficult in admitting they've been wrong.

The insist upon being the center of the spotlight.

Being aware that someone you care about might suffer from an inferiority disorder can aid in understanding the behavior of their. You may also be able help them overcome their obstacles and encourage them to seek professional help.

Chapter 4: How To Overcome Inferiority Complex?

Are you afraid of entering a venue or boardroom, or even your work place? There are many who experiences this. It's astonishing how common it is to be afflicted with an attitude of inferiority. A sense of inferiority According to psychiatrists, is a feeling that you are not good enough that is based on imagined or real reasons. In addition, since our inner critic loves taking on the form of our biggest adversary, much of it is constructed.

An inferiority complex can be defined as a false feeling of inadequacy in general, triggered by perceived or actual inferiority on one subject, usually associated with compensatory behavior.

Do you identify with this? Here's how you can remove it. Because it's possible!

"However, I do feel insufficient!"

Others are a source of anxiety during our daily lives which can make us feel insecure and insignificant. This can include everyone from bosses to lovers to people who are strangers at parties, famous people at school or in at work, and even famous people.

It's natural to feel like you've got something to prove yourself every now and then. People we love (or people who we don't know, but believe are awesome) are often able to rekindle the notion about whether we're competent enough, smart enough or intriguing enough. But the positive is that you're already there. Friends, we are all equal like there is no better animal or ocean or star in the night sky.

All of us are derived from the same place, regardless of our religious beliefs. Also, we are remarkably different from each other which means that each one person has something unique that we can contribute to conversations or in a social context (now should we believed and understood this, don't you think?)? !

If your inferiority complex resurfaces the ugly side of your head think about these essential facts:

1. You and not them who is to blame.

The fear of other people comes from inside us, not someone else. Recognizing this helps us let it go. If we feel like we are inferior to people, we're quick to judge. We raise their status to the level of superhuman and convince they are perfect. They have no flaws. They are all-knowing. Being aware that the cause is you thinking is the most effective method to get rid of it. This is not related to them in the slightest. You alone are the cause of your self-deflection.

2. Everyone has flaws, fears, and anxieties.

"I'm insecure and humble, and I embarrass myself," Jordan Belfort, the notorious Wolf of Wall Street, said in his memoir. However, I'm not going reveal the world that. I'd rather die than embarrassment when I had to pick between both. Therefore, I'm not perfect." Even the wolves get scared! all suffer from the feeling of being inadequate. This is one of the primary reasons that many celebrities suffer from addiction. Because of their inadequacy feelings and the imposter syndrome, they look for unsuitable ways of coping.

What exactly is impostor syndrome? precisely?

When we believe we don't deserve our achievements, we endure "Imposter Syndrome." We believe that we've fooled people to believe we're capable and we attribute our achievements to luck or luck. The inability to recognize our talents can make people feel as if we're a fake or fraud and could be in danger of being exposed. This is a horrible manifestation in the workplace of the mentality of inferiority.

Impoverer's syndrome, particularly prevalent among women who have high performance is not just a barrier from achieving our goals However, it also reduces our current potential. We avoid exciting opportunities and new concepts because we feel unworthy and inadequate. Many "what-might-have-been" are killed by imposter syndrome.

Does this describe you? It's very like the excuses I hear constantly (including from me)

3. Be aware that people are just that: human beings.

In three different instances I've found this to be true. Two of these were located in New York. One of those occasions was when I had the pleasure of meeting Kelsey Grammar. As an avid fan, something struck me and I walked up to Kelsey Grammar with just a an earful and my name. I also offered some words of appreciation for his efforts.

He was an excellent gentleman to be honest! Kelsey stood up from his seat and welcomed me into his home with his wife and thanked me for dropping by. His wife was equally pleasant.

The other occasion was when I was able to meet Rachael Ray in a dinner party. The same way I introduced myself, and I inquired about her work and what she was doing. She was pleasant and friendly and also shared with me her experience in the culinary industry. It's interesting to note that she's got no formal training, but has no inferiority complex! She's got it going.

It was interesting to me. Most people, even famous people are cool!

The third time was in 2007 when I offered my number to a beautiful stranger who was at an event in Sydney. He has since become my husband! If my sense of inadequacy were to be in charge that I could not only never be married to such a lovely man at the moment and I would be missing out on the joys of life. This isn't a good life!

4. Other people may be jittery too.

Hey, you're intimidating. Have you thought about the possibility? The term "shy" is often interpreted to mean being aloof. A few drinks later my friend who appeared distant confided to me that he's shy and likes the interaction with people around him because he is not confident in taking initiative.

If I said I thought he looked an aloof person and aloof, he was shocked since that was not his goal. You could remove two people's worries by making the first move in a social setting and greet them!

It's not necessary to make a fuss about your anxiety and feelings of unworthiness. Thinking that other people have the same feelings as that you do is often an appropriate and kind way to go. Concentrate on them. Let them feel comfortable. In just a couple of seconds, you'll be feeling at peace. Watch how fast your sense of insecurity disappears!

5. If you worry and stress you're giving your ego a boost.

The lower part of you is speaking to you through fear and anxiety. Or, you could say that you could be the "obnoxious roommate in your head... send them an eviction notice!" according to Arianna Huffington put it.

Who benefits by having an ego mind? Nobody. You can divert your attention when you're caught in an analytical insanity - or when your insecurities are growing - to become more affluent, less thin and more interesting. Get away from the problem. You can even switch on the TV or contact a kind and friendly acquaintance. Do not stay in that dangerous area! It is possible to change the location in a flash when you decide to move on.

"I choose peace instead of this," declares The Study in Miracles.

6. The feeling of being inadequate is removed by praise and love.

The feeling of being inferior disappears when we see others from the perspective of love, not fear. Therefore, the next time you are struck by something such as a friend who gets an excellent job, makes an unforgettable trip to Bali or buys a house or is engagedsend them your sincere congratulations. If good things happen to others, it implies that it is possible for it to occur to you too!

The accomplishments of someone else is not a reason to dismiss your own. It is possible to benefit from the achievements of other people. If you look at success in the right light and viewed in the right way, it proves that getting the goals we desire is achievable for everyone. Alexis's physique was changed through an exercise routine that included barre and her coworker was also in the studio and benefited from Alexis her months of study! The colleague would have been shut from this amazing benefit if she was from a perspective of comparison , rather than one of the desire to learn and be open.

7. Get involved!

It is always possible to put your focus on what you already have instead of what others have , by focusing on the things you possess. This puts the inferiority part to hidden background, out of sight and in the back of your mind. Think about it this way: if you were have a crush on anyone, would you wish to be a part of their lives as well? Perhaps not. If I'm exhausted and am waiting on the line for a while, or when my subway is running late I love to look back at the elements of my life I cherish at the time. It's been the dreaded fall for some time. The month of October I'll be spending time with my mom at home in The United Kingdom.

On Sundays, I'll be viewing Game of Thrones (HBO) and re-reading Gay Hendricks' life-changing book The Big Leap, and drinking my husband's brand new bulletproof coffee that I make for him every morning.

If you are looking for it, you will find plenty of happiness to be found in your life! It's impossible to be humble and grateful simultaneously. Say goodbye to your self-defeating ego!

8. If you're concerned If you're worried, think about "What's the worst that may happen?"

A person could run into you. What's the problem? 'So what?' is among the most crucial questions you could ask yourself. I've been to a lot of networking and pitching events during my 10-year career in sales and have been dismayed more than I can recall. I'm still active and healthy, so far as I'm aware (and definitely more successful because of continuing to pursue it). Being unique requires that you be vulnerable sometimes. Being willing to take risks that others don't is an essential aspect of success. This means letting go of your insecurity and taking things less serious!

Keep in mind that God is kind and wants you to be able to achieve everything you want. If you're afraid it blocks the flow of possibilities and creativity, as well as the miraculous events. Instead, focus your energy on remembering who you are when you're at your best and most optimum?

9. Don't get too serious about your life.

When I was a teenager waitress in a cafe, the proprietor was strict about it. If we fell on glass or a plate then we were required to laugh over it! It was a great policy. But, recently I was cursing at my ceiling (loudly) while I walked around my apartment after I sent an email that contained an in error link, and then having to send the same email to around 40,00 people who live in my neighborhood with apology and the right link.

It would appear that I was suffering from heart attacks If you were a flies in the wall. What went wrong? Nothing. "It's good to know you're human!" Someone even wrote me.

Ha. Do you have the ability to make your laugh a bit louder? A sense of humor is the ideal remedy to feelings of insecurity and self-deflection.

10. What is the most ideal scenario?

This is an amazing question. What happens if this does come out? This is my title in my new book.

This is among the most intriguing questions we could ever ask! The possibilities are endless. It is possible to create a new friendship and establish a new professional relationship, or meet a potential date! If we let the fear of failure and that constant inferiority mindset to control our lives, there are plenty of opportunities. Believe that positive expectations have the power to change lives. What if all your thoughts were focused on the outcome you wanted? It's not hard to figure out how!

11. Do not take things too seriously.

Take a look at Don Miguel Ruiz's work, The Four Agreements, if you're seeking some peace as well as bliss and heck yes! Power in your life. Because, well you're very and you are and well, well it's not going to change your life in the same way as this one when you are suffering from an inferiority complex. should be taken personal.

A friend's last-minute cancellation? Oh well. Interviews that didn't go well? Next. Are you ever disappointed by an acquaintance? This is also fine. This isn't about me at all.

The reality is that everything you do by other people is because of you! People's actions and words reflect their personal reality and their personal experience. When we act as a victim and feel devalued and unable to understand, we have no idea of what's happening to others. You won't be the cause of unnecessary anxiety and stress if you are not averse to the thoughts and behavior of others. Not at all. If you don't take things personally, you can enjoy an immense amount of freedom. It's like you're receiving the most effective medicine in the world! There's no more bind to any limitations!!

12. Learn to practice self-compassion.

The most effective form of self-help is self-compassion. Get it from a self-help guru like me. Let's say that you made an error -- no problem! What was the result? There's no reason to allow your self-defeating tendencies to come back up time and again. Think about this: what did I discover? The majority of errors (slip-ups) are helpful to us, as they can teach us something. There isn't way to live a flawless existence, so you should learn from every little mistake. Do you quickly and graciously apologize if you think you've made a mistake and then find out the truth? In other words, why not allow it to go? Just let it be human and move on to your next thing to do?

13. Release the illusion of perfection.

It's possible that we all could be kinder to ourselves? Why do we have a need to be doing everything in a precise manner, whether it's eating healthy all the time, or making sure that our personal blog posts aren't full of grammar errors? Nothing can exacerbate our insecurity as the false assumption that we need to be perfect in any way.

I was eating breakfast with a friend who wanted to begin blogging, but let her perfectionist tendencies hinder her. It prevented her from starting an online blog initially.

"You know what's helping me push past my block?" she inquired. The entire week, I go through your blog posts even if they contain some spelling errors. Simply decide to write it down!"

It's true! If I do make mistakes, I am able to apologize to myself. Because it's amazing being human. Your mistakes (like my spelling mistakes) may even be a source of inspiration for others! What's the point? "Done is better than perfect," Sheryl Sandberg said and I'm with her. Amen.

14. Control your thoughts

CONSUME UPLIFTING CONTENT ON A DAILY BASIS IS A HUGE SOURCE OF JOY FOR ME.

How can anyone survive without self-help books, informative podcasts, or inspirational blog posts?? I notice if I skip a single day. It allows me to remain in the present moment and assert my personal power and release my self-deprecating mindset. The inner inspiration of my mind is highly influenced by external inspiration.

The need for this book clearer to me than when someone told me that last year they believed I was scary prior to meeting me. What's up, me? Me, the girl-from-a-small-town who is super pleasant, petite, and constantly smiling? The characteristics that scare us vary from person to person the same way that our expectations. "No one can make you feel inferior without your cooperation," declared Eleanor Roosevelt, and this is a universal fact. You don't have to see you in person to understand the fact that I, your friend is not inferior.

Chapter 5: Peer Pressure

What is Peer Pressure?

Peer pressure occurs when a person is influenced by a peer group or individual to adhere to a defined standard of behaviour or conduct. If someone is made to feel pressured to change their behaviour as well as their thinking and actions due to the influence of others is a part of the concept of peer pressure.

Most often, children take on the words or actions as well as practices from their peers. This could be anything from swear words and smoking as well as after-school studying as well as co-curricular activities. That's why it is important to be aware that peer pressure comes composed of two types.

Positive Peer Pressure

Positive peer pressure occurs the moment when someone gives up negative behavior and bad habits or takes up positive behaviour. For instance when a child ceases using foul or offensive language due to the fact that his/her peers aren't using such words, then that is an example of positive peer pressure.

Negative Peer Pressure

Negative peer pressure happens the time when someone abandons positive habits and/or adopts bad habits because of their environment and people. A good example could be when students in high school pick up smoking cigarettes because their friends request that they try it, or when the child ceases working on extra credit since it's not cool according to their classmates.

Does peer pressure really exist? thing?

Yes! It is definitely real and a lot of us are victims. Whatever age or old, it is very easy to be influenced by the opinions of our peers and anyone else in our vicinity.

Sometimes peer pressure is explicit, for example, the person who asks you to go to an alcoholic drink because they are cool. But, other times it's quite subtle and doesn't need to be announced publicly to achieve the desired effect. It is entirely possible for someone to feel influenced by all in their vicinity without needing to assert that the behavior and actions of that person is wrong or in error.

Signs of Peer Pressure

Peer pressure can be very insignificant and hard to recognize in some children, yet it can be very obvious in other. For parents who are vigilant it's easy to recognize indications that their child is becoming a victim to peer pressure, typically by noticing the following indicators:

1. Unexpectedly sudden changes in the way you conduct yourself or behaviors and even beliefs.

2. The risk of developing a chronic illness is greatly increased.

3. The signs and evidence of abuse.

4. Unscrupulous behavior is usually classified as inappropriate and out of character.

5. The signs of depression.

6. A new group of friends is forming for your children.

7. Distracting or secretive demeanor.

8. The sudden focus is on the the image.

9. Academic performance changes.

10. Try or do things which were usually boring or boring prior to.

In the event that any of these symptoms are noticed at an early age the child could be prevented from developing an insecurity disorder.

What causes peer pressure to lead into the development of an Inferiority Complex?

We've already discussed the concept the existence of two kinds of pressure from peers. But, the focus of this book is on the ways in which negative peer pressure could lead to the creation of an inferiority complex within a child.

Teenagers, children as well as the general population around us are often harsh in their critique of another. Someone must conform to a particular standard of appearance, speech and acting to be accepted as a member of a particular group in society. The same is true for children. the moment children think they are different from others who are "cooler" and possess more influential and social benefits, they begin to view themselves as less than. This leads to the formation of an "inferiority" complex that has a myriad of negative impacts on a child's psychological physical, emotional, and mental well-being.

Chapter 6: Understanding Inferiority

The psychological concept, the Inferiority complex which was first described in the 1920s by Alfred Alder in 1920s, is a sense of inferiority that an individual experiences about himself in comparison to others.

An inferiority complex can be described as an insufficiency of self-worth, uncertainty, doubt and doubt, as well as the feeling of not living with the standards. It's usually hidden and it is believed to cause sufferers to compensate for their condition which can result in either a dramatic success or extreme behavior in social settings.

An inferiority complex typically stems from real, imaginary or in-built feelings of being inferior. In the majority of cases, there is a mix of the imagination and subtle conditioning. The feeling of inferiority occurs when a circumstance makes them feel inferior to others, and their imaginative thinking alters their reactions and perception of the situation beyond what would be normal to someone else.

The idea of self-esteem as an inferior person is not an intrinsic characteristic. No one is born with the desire to be less than oneself. it's the circumstances and the environment, people, and the environment that cause a person to lower himself to the level of other people. There is no way to be born feeling inferior , so how can we fall into feelings of being inadequate? Our lives and our culture instil in us the notion that we are not worthy. There are societies that consider as much, even to the point of religion, success as well as money and beauty. The constant focus on these things instills youngsters' minds on a regular basis. This causes the people living in the same society to always look at their own lives in comparison to others.

Inferiority is taught to people by society, even if they have some of the resources that the society expects and wants. The worldly and material things are part of this, but most people are offended by their appearance. Dark skin, curly eyes, flaked cheeks fat body, wrinkled neck All of these make people feel inferior to those that aren't too concerned about the opinions of others.

The majority of people eventually recognize the differences among the members of their peers. It's a crucial realization that we're not created equal. Children are born having physical injury, defects and diseases. Furthermore, not all birth parent will have the financial resources to address these challenges. But, everyone can benefit from his or her strengths, as well as their weaknesses.

The child's position in the family's group significantly influences the self-image of a child and their sense of superiority or insignificant to other children. The children in the early years of school start to form different groups of friends in the kindergarten years. After each grade, schoolmates begin to make people feel welcomed or rejected as being distinct by their friends.

From a very early age, the basic elements of hate towards other people are instilled into children by their parents. "Don't play with that dirty boy' that dirty boy gets a bad rap and after a while, the child who was offended offers motivational talks to the dirty boys to not feel less worthy.

The Inferiority Complex could also be described as an issue in the desires to be noticed as a worthy person and the fear or fear to be humiliated.

Signs Of Inferiority Complex

These are the indicators that alert us to stop people from being slighted.

Social Withdrawal

They don't like being part of crowds due to the fact that they cannot remove the sneaking feeling that they aren't quite as competent as the other. They'd rather not let other people find out about how weak or unsecure they really are. They would rather be alone.

Place Own Needs Last

A feeling of inferiority could cause people to put their requirements first. In reality, they're struggling with feelings of being unworthy. In the course of time they begin to build up anger.

Procrastination

They don't seem to be motivated. There's a reason they can't leave the couch. The underlying belief is that regardless of how hard they do, they're not sufficient.

Sensitivity To Criticism

Even though people who feel inadequate "know" they have shortcomings but they don't want people who point this out. They generally view any criticism, no matter how kindly or constructively portrayed in a way, as a personal attack.

Hypercritical Attitude (H.P)

Individuals who don't feel confident about themselves will find it difficult to feel positive about others. They are constantly looking for faults and flaws of other people convincing themselves they aren't that bad at all. People who are like this don't feel confident, intelligent beautiful, capable and so on. as long as they're the most attractive, intelligent and knowledgeable person around.

Inappropriate Response To Flattery

It can be done in two ways. Certain people are eager to hear positive things about themselves, and are always looking for praises. Others might be hesitant to hear anyone who is positive about themselves as it doesn't align with their personal feelings.

Tendency Towards Blaming (T.T.B.)

A few people project their shortcomings on others in order to ease and lessen the pain and humiliation of being inferior. For example when someone reveals his flaws or inadequacy other people in order to cause them to be aware of it, so that their perceived incompetence is justified by a story of misery. This is simply a way toward delegating the responsibility for their shortcomings to someone else.

Feeling Of Persecution (F.O.P.)

If carried to the point of extreme, the blame game can lead to the belief that other people are actively seeking to harm their lives. If students fail on an exam and is unable to pass, he may be resigned to believe that the teacher is not happy and will take any action to hurt him. This can only help him to escape personal responsibility for his actions.

Sensitivity To Criticism (S.T.C.)

Even though people who feel inadequate know they are flawed but they don't want others to point these out. They often view any criticism, no matter how gently and constructively addressed in a way, as a personal attack.

Tendency Towards Seclusion and Sensitivity (T.T.S.S.)

Because those with an inferiority complex feel that they're not as smart or interesting as their peers, they assume others have the same feelings about their own abilities and intelligence. Therefore, they not speak up in public due to the fear that it will result in an embarrassing display of their lack of knowledge.

Negative Feeling About Competition (N.F.A.C.)

People who suffer from inferiority are more likely winning contests and games like everyone else, but they are unable to win in any circumstances because they know that they will never be able to get ahead. Being last is a clear sign of failing.

Effects Of Inferiority Complex

The inferiority complex can make people feel like an unintentional stone that is their own persona. They begin to lose their origins, and what they are a part of. If a child is afflicted by the specter of inadequacy the performance of his be lacking. Whatever you do, he will lose because he feels alone in a world in which his confidence is a shattered mirror. The performance of his is beginning to diminish and the feeling of inferiority engulfs the entirety of his existence.

As a person who is deemed inferior The only thing he focuses on is on the negative aspects of himself and in his life. He can't even think of a comfortable life or family, which is why his health is deteriorating. The behavior of the man is getting worse with every day. They do not value the people is around them, and their disrespect becomes an attribute in their behavior. His relationships and connections have a sour taste. He sees everything else in a sour and depressing glass. He considers himself an unworthy person and without dignity.

It's normal to feel that you are inferior to someone else, but when this feeling takes control of someone's actions and causes feelings of depression that blocks regular life activities, it's a sign of having an inferiority complex. It is crucial to discover the source of your developed feelings of inferiority in your life. They could be simply an untruth you believed regarding yourself as a result of poor childhood experiences must be examined and considered your surroundings and the those who taught your.

Therefore, we conclude that the concept of inferiority results in misunderstandings within our society. It can be detrimental to children and adults an emotional point viewpoint and in many other factors. The Inferiority Complex must be addressed in a respectful and equal manner. To ensure that they succeed, learn effectively, and develop the minds of their children in a trauma-free condition.

Chapter 7: Root Causes of Inferiority Complex

We've been there. Being a bit inferior to a friend or a cousin, or even an older sibling. The feeling of inferiority is when we believe that other people around us are more superior than us and are smarter, more productive and more happy. This causes feelings of anger among people. However, the majority instances of these are short-lived. In the end, we will find something else to be thankful for, and the feelings fade away. However, sometimes, people are unable to remove these emotions which can lead to an insecurity. However, there is be a reason why some individuals are more likely to be affected by these emotions. We've tried to find out the root causes of an insecurity and inferiority complex among individuals, and some of the root causes have been explored below.

Financial Background

It is a typical reason for feeling of inadequacy within the population. Your relatives may be richer. You may be friends with people who are financial secure are, or who own better vehicles and be feeling like you're not living your life style. In the end, they've done it better than you. If you keep going in this direction it's very easy to be entangled in feelings of anger and anger. Then the feelings you feel aren't hurting anyone else other than you. In the end, you're suffering because you feel that you're not a good enough person compared to the people in your life.

Childhood Trauma

A child's childhood is the time when a person is exposed to the most. Any emotional turmoil at this point can be detrimental to an individual, even after they grow up to become an adult. Psychologists believe that the reason why some individuals aren't confident in their professional life, is due to the fact that they did not get the proper direction when they were children. They also were criticized by their parents as bad examples for their children to emulate, or who played favoritism with their children. This is why, in the present, their childhoods have affected the development of their personalities.

Low Self Esteem

A lack of self-esteem is a much more frequent issue than we imagine. There are many people who have talent, potential and resources, but they're not able to make a difference because they don't believe in themselves. They aren't sure they'll be able to do the same things as those can accomplish. Fear of failure causes low self-esteem. People are afraid of trying new things due to the fact that they don't believe they'll do efficiently, and thus be unable to succeed. This creates an insecurity that hinders a person to achieve their potential.

Clinical Depression

Depressed people are also more likely to be into an inferiority disorder. They tend to be in a circle and are constantly focused on their issues, but not trying to come up with solutions. If someone is depressed, they begin to compare themselves to other people around them. They also begin to believe that other people have a better life than they do in their lives, in their relationships, and even at work. The inferiority complex deprives people of the confidence which is essential to break rid of depressive symptoms.

Pampered Lifestyle

Children who have grown up being able to have everything taken care of cannot think things through independently. After they graduate and begin to live their own lives, they're not sure how to handle the challenges that adulthood presents to them. Parents and relatives have been awed themto the point that they don't know how to think independently. When they fall short they aren't sure the reason why they're doing wrong. Instead, they observe that their peers can complete the tasks with ease, but they can't get grasp of. This can lead to self-recrimination which leads them to believe that they're incapable to make it in the world.

Social Disadvantage

Because of economic, social and political factors many people are confused in their lives. Or, they were born into a family which is poor on the social scale or belong to an ethnic group that doesn't get the benefits it should get. While this may be unfair, they are prone to thinking that they should be treated this manner. They begin thinking that certain individuals are more fortunate, not because they are unfair however, they believe that they are superior to others. This is why an inferiority complex develops. The resulting complex can undermine their personal struggle and, as a result, they're never satisfied with their own self-esteem. If they're not sure, they can not believe that good things will occur to them. Therefore, they'll reduce their expectations for themselves.

Understanding the Causes of these and their elimination

Each of these causes is true. Yet, most people aren't aware to the real reason why they're experiencing a problem. It is crucial to understand that any problem is able to be identified to allow us to proceed to resolve the issue in a manner that actually works. If you attempt to get rid of your insecurity this will benefit you over the long term. Your life will turn out towards a more optimistic outlook, and an improvement is likely to occur. The majority of people don't try to resolve this issue the correct method. They believe they can beat their addiction having more money, or luxury items. However, in the end they're even more desperate as this comfort will only last for a few days. When the initial joy of purchasing something vanishes and they realize that it wasn't the thing they were looking for at all.

Therefore, before you decide to solve the issue it is important to comprehend the root cause. Also, you must remove it from its source. Here are some questions that you could ask yourself.

Why do I feel this like this?

You should consider whether there is a valid reason to feel superior to other people. Are they working harder than you? Are they more intelligent? Or is it just luck? Perhaps it's something financial which is making you be this way. Perhaps, you're depressed and you're not able to focus your thoughts. It is crucial to understand the reason you're experiencing this type of feeling, or else you'll be unable to eliminate the issue out of your daily life. Becauseuntil you are aware of the reason for why you experience this feeling, you will not be able to determine how to get out of it.

What can I do to resolve this issue?

In the next step, you need to ask your own approach to solving the issue. Understanding the issue is one thing, but how to approach it is a different. Can it be improved if you alter your habits, or attempt to exercise more or eat healthier? Perhaps you should go to therapy due to behaviors that hurt your health in the end. There's a lengthy list of issues but the majority of them are solvable. The most important thing is that you're committed and perseverant to work on the issues. There are quite a number of ways this can be accomplished.

First of all, you must to stay busy. It has been observed that people think more positively when they are doing their best. Anyone with a lot of free time will discover it easy to slip into negative thought patterns. This is an obstacle.

Then, get assistance from your friends. Ask them if they've encountered something similar. If yes, how did they resolve the issue? Perhaps they have helpful tips to offer. If they aren't able to offer advice, they'll be able to listen and often, it's all a person requires.

* Thirdly, you should try to come up with new ideas for your future. Even if your previous plans weren't working out the way you expected they would, you need to begin somewhere. If you are able to anticipate higher quality things, greater circumstances could come your way.

* Fourthly, forget your past failures. Learn from them, but don't think about them throughout your day. They're designed to impart wisdom and not deter you from making your life to the fullest.

Finally, it is vital to have confidence in yourself. If you're confident about your abilities, you'll boost your chances of happiness. If you don't believe in yourself, you'll fall short in the tasks you could have accomplished easily.

Chapter 8: Prevention Is Better Than Cure

The saying goes "prevention is better than cure" "prevention is better than cure" We will discuss ways we can stop such events or the reasons that make the flowers of weakness to develop within our bodies. It is true that nothing is insurmountable or unchangeable. Life continues. People move forward. The degree of extremism increases and is just therefore, the degree of superiority or inferiority in one's life can grow or diminish too. There are many ways to combat it, but how do we bring the disease into our lives when we could prevent it?

A bit difficult to grasp right now? So, do you wish to be comfortably in your skin, or do you would like to remove it and replace it in a great deal of discomfort? It could be natural, but humans are naturally created and are nature. We are the creators of our own causalities and neutralities.

The meaning of the quotation is that it's always simpler to avoid the issue instead of having to deal with it at all. It is important to use our capacity to see ahead and attempt to avoid any negative situation that might be a possibility in the future. We must be vigilant enough to implement all necessary precautions to reduce the risk of a particular situation.

If we plan our actions well and are prepared, we're more likely to see positive outcomes from our actions. Because we've prepared it properly and have a clear mind, we will be at peace. So , prepare to master how to manage the pesky bugger off your shoulders for good once and for all.

Are you ready kids? "Aye Aye Captain"

I'm not able to hear you! "AYE AYE CAPTAIN"

This is great! Let's go now. Everyone aboard! !

The train is about to leave...chu chu chuchigchigchig...chu chu...

Okay, the first thing we're going to cover in this chapter is to avoid inferiority complex. After we have finished with that, we'll be sure to are able to show off your self-esteem!

Ready? Okay, good.

How to avoid developing inferiority complex:

Acceptance:

Accept things for what they are. Don't attempt to change the laws of nature. What happens if a person scores more marks than you do in the same test? Everyone has their individual strengths. It's not the same for everyone. Don't consider yourself to be something less. Are you aware that the field of psychology has proposed an idea in which the different types of intelligence are described? Based on the concept of "multiple intelligence", there are nine different kinds of intelligence. Each of these types of intelligence corresponds to a completely different perception of one's personality and the interests of one's.

So, if anyone ever says you're dumb or unintelligent, simply inform them to clarify their beliefs. However, before you do that, take the time to accept the world and people in the way they are. There is nothing and nobody superior to you. We all are the same. Although we may not be able to excel in the same way, however, our various types of intelligences enrich us as well as our surroundings. It's like the entire human race is a body and we are merely body parts performing our individual functions...just as our human body has parts that are all part of the earth's body herself! !

Aim high and learn to focus:

Everyone has something great and we only need the eye to be able to see it! The thing you must understand initially is that we're identical and if we are willing to try, to be as successful as the billionaires in existence to the present. It is important to grasp the fact that there's the winner in every person! It's all about the importance of. When the child you refer to as the nerd has a preference for studying, and you are more concerned with having a good time at the same time, a distinction is made. He devotes his time to studying in order to get the goals he has set when you're still playing. If someone is scoring more than you do, you can go through the background of the many fun activities they have done and then add the things you've done. You'll have an answer to refer to whenever you're not making a priority of your goals.

As with your lover or crush...your goals also require your attention, as well as plenty of time! The person who is a winner in you is not difficult to spot once you have set to the road to reach your goals and realize your desires. The winner is only subdued or weakened by moments of fear or losing interest in the being bored with the subject. If you are feeling like this is happening, recall the reason that sparked the fire within you to pursue your goal initially. Once you've remembered it will assist you in regaining your belief and the motivation behind it instead of deconstructing your "to be accomplished" lists.

Reach your goal:

Get rid of boredom because it will hinder you in no way. It will not just make you stop, but also lure you into the desire to relax all day with nothing to do but let you fall off the path. Remember that 'all fun and no work make Jack dull' . From now on, it doesn't matter if you're bored with your day-to-day chores or simply overwhelmed by your goals Once you allow it to go...it disappears. You'll be left with nothing but poof as well as the new life you've begun millennium ago. Our origins were as monkeys, but our fascination with nature brought new and innovative concepts into our minds. If we'd stopped in that moment, no progress would have happened to humans. We'd still be in a cave, with a few scratches on our bodies in order to conceal our riches, and that's the only evolutionary step for us until now. Constantness is an essential requirement for those who want to accomplish something. You should anticipate or be expected to defend your choice before your loved ones and family at the moment it is time. The ability to remain constant and indestructible is what brings about constantness and brings joy to life.

You're beautiful!

"I see humans wanting to be attractive and desirable nowadays! I've heard of people who are spending hours in the hopes of being attractive to the entire world. I've heard that they are always busy with cosmetics and procedures. They aren't well-aware of is you'll be gorgeous the moment you begin becoming yourself!"

Do not!! Don't go to feeling ugly or bad when someone has a more beautiful skin tone or voice. You are beautiful as you are. You don't have to hide from the world wondering if people will see you for being ugly. People whom make you feel this way do it only because they are under the pressure to be superior to them. Smile, be authentic and let go of all the negativity that surround you. You are someone they consider interesting enough that they would like for you to feel guilty. They only do this when they feel uneasy about the presence of you. So , just chill and take in the spectacle.

Interpersonal or Intrapersonal?

Interpersonal intelligence means having an understanding of those around you , which makes it more palatable and easy to get along with nearly everyone Intrapersonal intelligence is having a deep understanding of one's self. It's not a huge problem if the majority of us have the ability to communicate with others that oozes from our bodies because we'd only be able to understand the needs of fellow people. What we really need is a clearer and better understanding of our own personal wants and needs. The confusions that occupy our minds frequently cause chaos and confusion within our souls. We continue to challenge ourselvesat times due to our shaky personal knowledge. All you have to do is study and be your own best friend. Be aware of your feelings and put away your confusion and indecisiveness. Take yourself seriously. Own you!

How to boost your spirits:

Breathe:

If you are feeling down about something, take the entire thing into. Inhale all the negative and melancholic feelings or thoughts that make you feel like hell. You are more powerful than your sorrow; always was and always will be! There is no one who can stop you over time except for you on the other side of the spectrum. Inhale all the negativity surrounding you and connect with your inner monsters. Ask yourself as many questions as you want to. Ask yourself the time you want to...because trying to escape from a situation or putting your thoughts out into your unconscious would do nothing to aid in any way. Nobody would be able to judge you! Nobody has the right to. However, if they do it's because his life is boring or useless due to the fact that his sole way to entertain himself is watching you. They pay attention because that is the only purpose they're given within their own lives. The sun is the only thing that can be seen for their dying planet , and regardless of how much we dislike seeing the sun shining in the summer months, we look forward to the cold winter days to pass with the sole purpose of watching the sun shine in its full splendor.

Believe:

There is no need to be perfect. All you have to do is trust. Believe in the future and even for worse to come. Believe in the knightly sun to rise every dark night, and avoid all dark shadows returning to their own world. Believe since once you stop doing this, you will not be able to think of it once more. It would be impossible to see the beauty in your surroundings. You will never be able to live a life without believing. Simply believe in the power of positive forces and positive things will be coming your way.

There is no need to feel bad about the villain. Look deep and believe that it is a good person. You will soon know why he's how you see him. There is no one who is truly good or bad, it's dependent on the people of the world to mold their character to become either a hero or a villain. Our care level can transform a character into an antagonist, and the reverse. Therefore, just because something isn't working, it doesn't necessarily mean that you have lost confidence in or trust in the outcome.

Revenge?

Someone has hurt you in a terrible way and you now want to take revenge to please your ego? You considered them to be acquaintances, but then they revealed your blindness? You'd like to feel exactly the same way or perhaps even greater than you felt?

We've all had similar experiences. We all had plans for an attack on our most hated foes among our social circle of friends. We all are frustrated by teachers being a constant nuisance on our daily lives. We laugh with them along with our peers. We slam them on their backs, hoping that we, or our significant other may feel more comfortable. There is no one to judge you!

There is no one who can...because everyone is guilty of this. If you judge yourself for feeling this way or thinking this way on behalf of someone else is like saying we're judging ourselves, and we don't want to do that is it? Everyone hates having their fingers that are pointed in the other's direction, isn't it? Relax and take a breath. Let's face it, 99.5% humans spend their lives seeking revenge and creating ideal scenarios in their minds in order to retaliate against the people who caused them to feel down at first.

When your thoughts are focused on people all day long, it's like he's yours isn't he? It is a pleasure to talk negative things about them. The thought of revenge and its repercussions relaxes your mind and boosts your mood. Although you're not part of someone else's life the fact that you spend half your time creating ideal scenarios inside the walls of your mind. This is a reference of being dependent on them within your thoughts. It's impossible to not be thinking about them do you? How do you get rid of them? What is your peace? Even if you're not part of "them you are an element of you. Do you think it's fair? be fair?

It's true that it's unfair and we are aware that it will never be fair when it comes to the issue being in dispute, but this is when you are faced with a crucial issue to consider. You must ask yourself whether you would rather think for the rest of your life about someone who is as unimportant as them , or do you want to feel at peace? Indeed, revenge is the only thing that makes you happy, but you'd never find peace.

So, if you have someone who has been a problem for you, simply release it. You're not able to be able to bring yourself down to the level of theirs. You're not cool enough to be able to respond. Do you know that whenever an lion sits, dogs are able to come up and bark at it , but it never responds to their calls. Why? Because he's the lion...the

King. He isn't concerned about how his servants conduct themselves. Don't be a lion! Make sure you are a courageous cat! !

Chapter 9: Climbing The Ladder

To conquer the inferiority complex To overcome the inferiority complex, you must understand that you are able to become the very best. You're not less than the people you admire. All your dreams and goals are possible. But, to become the most successful requires certain changes on your behalf. You must take specific steps that allow you to become the person you wish to be.

One of the primary reasons that cause inferiority develops is the fact that we see our self in a negative light. We are critical of ourselves, regardless of whether anyone else has to. Making excuses for our shortcomings and talking to ourselves about the mistakes we commit, can hinder our progress towards becoming the most perfect. The first step should be not telling ourselves you're not good enough. Do not stare in the mirror and wonder what you could have done to look better or how unassuming you appear. Do not worry about whether your dress sense is not perfect.

Don't think that the work you performed was of poor quality. Don't dwell on the idea that you are incompetent. Once you have stopped thinking about all the negative thingsabout yourself, you'll realize the fact that everything you thought was negative was a mistake by you. Be aware that your appearance, character, your skills as well as your virtues and talents can be regarded as among the top. The issue is not on you, it's in the way you are thinking.

Eliminating the negative thoughts that you're not enough doesn't erase the negativity is necessary to shake of. The other thing to do is not judge people. It is important to be aware of your judgemental mindset in order to be the most effective. Do not judge other people just based on how they appear. Making assumptions or expressing negative opinions about others can result in you falling instead of rising. Recognize that even as you're struggling, other have a similar struggle , and you have to respect this. Try to let the most of your negative energy leave your body as much as you can.

Once you've made the decision to accept yourself as you are and feel satisfied with your self The next step needs to be to avoid letting any fear be a barrier for you. The fear of failing and the fear of success hinder our abilities and attempt to hinder our progress towards the success we desire. The assumption that you will never attain your goal, and thinking that it's beyond the level you can achieve will not allow you to succeed. Everyone is capable of reaching their goals.

There's no reason why you aren't successful in obtaining what you want when you do your best. The chance of not getting it lies solely in your mind. This fear isn't letting you perform to the fullest. This makes you do lesser than you would be able to do without anxiety. It is important to be aware that the anxiety about failure is simply an assumption and is a reason that makes your work less efficient. So, it is best to avoid it at all cost.

A fear that comes with success is when you think that because all is well it must be something that isn't right. When you're performing to the best of your ability and things seem to be moving in the direction you want Being convinced that something could be wrong can cause it to go wrong in one way or another. It happens because you are trying to find a flaw, then you perform something that will make your belief prove true. In truth, if your anxiety of failure had not been present then there was no obstacle. There would not have been any lapses to your success. A fear of success is overcome by determination to achieve success. Be confident that nothing will be wrong and that everything will be corrected. Don't let anxiety cloud your determination.

When you've let go of your worries you're now able to maximize your potential without any obstacles or distraction, it is vital to focus your efforts towards achieving this goal. The most important thing to remember to remember is to never attempt to please others. While you want to stand out before others individuals, you'd like to be appreciated and would like them to be impressed by yourself, you should not attempt to conform to their wishes. Being yourself is the most important thing.

It's nearly impossible to please everyone since each has a only a majority of them are in agreement. Each person has their individual preferences and dislikes preferences, personal taste, ideas and perspectives. If you attempt to please everyone, you'll be unable to achieve it due to the conflicting opinions that come from their decisions. The best thing to do is take the steps you think are best. The importance of pleasing people isn't so much because once you're your own person and are confident the people will eventually accept the person you are if done your best to remove negative thoughts and inculcate positive qualities.

It is simple to talk about, however applying them requires a huge amount of effort and hard work. Being one of the top isn't easy. The act of putting off your goals can ruin any goals and hopes. If you don't work for it with all your heart and persevere the goal is likely to remain a dream instead of becoming a reality. It is vital to never let your hopes go down regardless of the length of time. It is essential to put in the effort for a long time. If your efforts fail in any way due to delay, all of the efforts you have put into them are at stake.If you do nothing and think about the improvements, they won't occur. Insanity will not permit you to achieve anything, therefore, get started today and make sure you put in your best effort. Don't waste time.

If a child does the best effort to rid himself of an inferiority disorder it is likely that the child will be able combat it eventually. But it could take a long time , and times, he is unable to take on the weight all by himself. In the current world we live in, it's not exaggerated to say that children are afflicted by the burden of difficulties in the same way as adults do. They may need help from a professional when things begin to spiral out of their control. It isn't wise to think that children do not have to see psychiatrists. They have to see an audiologist more often than adults.

The stage of childhood is in which you go through rapid shifts. The process of learning often too rapid to keep up with during this crucial time, there are many occurrences that can make you shake. Stress can be unbearable. In these instances, the symptoms must be monitored closely. If the child is beginning to withdraw himself from social interaction, or if he's engaging in aggressive behavior, participating into physical fights or is prone to drug abuse or suicidal ideas, has eating disorders, isn't doing well in school or other extracurricular activities, has difficulty concentrating, is overwhelmed by panic attacks or other drastic changes, it is essential to see psychiatrist.

Most children aren't able to express themselves, and parents do not understand their. The inferiority complex is a thing which children tend to keep from the outside. The issue is that children are unable to handle it on their own. They are still young and emotionally not resilient. Thus, a visit to a psychiatrist is a must. The psychiatrist is able to treat the anxieties and complicated issues of children. He can also provide guidance to parents on how to handle their child. The combined effort could produce remarkable results.

Inferiority-related complex among children is not something that is common, but the treatment of it is rare. If it isn't addressed in the early stages of the early years, it will grow over time and become more severe for adults, which can make life very difficult. The steps to be taken and practical methods of help from professionals must be mastered in order to defeat it. Inferiority complex may end completely. It's not something that can be cured. The following guidelines will assist children and allow them to become better adults.

Chapter 10: A Step in Building Your Self Confidence

There must be a starting point for all things. You will have to suffer incessantly from the very thing you are afraid of--lack of self-confidence--unless you get serious about improving your confidence.

Our responses to the events of our lives and the way in which we were shaped by the elders of our community and the way in which society views each of us contributes to confidence in ourselves. The perception of confidence we have about ourselves depends on a range of factors.

How satisfied we feel with the expectations we have of ourselves and the situations in our lives is a element. Expectations that are unrealistic are a frequent error made by a lot of people. The losses they suffer are getting too overwhelming for them to take on and, as a result they begin to lose confidence in their own abilities.

However there are those who prefer to be secure and set feasible, achievable objectives. In addition, they are more confident because they know the fact that they're in a way capable of achieving their goals and their achievements play a major part in the process.

You may have experienced the phrase "it's everything in your mind. "In addition that, in the case of various emotional and mental disorders it is possible to say that mind's at the heart of all things. Because they originate and are shaped by the mind, solutions may originate from the same place.

There is always the possibility of forming yourself to feel how you'd like or how you do not want to feel. It is possible to help feelings manifest and suppress the feelings. If you say that you would like to hate yourself for not feeling adequate. It will only result in two outcomes: true hate and lower self-esteem, If you believe in the hatred and believe that you're not enough.

When we speak, many individuals are caught off-guard. Sometimes, we don't determine if what we're thinking is actually registering in our unconscious mind.

Even though you may not have planned to say it in the past however, your subconscious may likely believe that these claims are real because you're used to hearing yourself say things such as "I am a looser" or "I am not worthy of anything."

These claims are supported by a vast majority of people around the world today.

They're not just words. They're real, and they'll get deep into your mind, and eventually be embedded in your brain. You cannot possibly be convinced of their opposite , if you believe in these.

Self-belief is a crucial element of self-confidence. Your preconceived ideas are accepted as truth. So, all you have to do is change the beliefs you wish to attain. If you don't, you'll never alter no regardless of how long. You must be the primary source of motivation.

While suggestions can originate from other sources, ultimately it will be your responsibility to take on the fight.

Changes must begin at the beginning of your own life. You can begin with telling yourself that, "You are great," because you're an amazing person waiting for your abilities to be utilized. Also, "you are beautiful" (because regardless of regardless of whether you believe it or not, every one of us was designed in a beautiful way to glorify the Creator).

If you don't have confidence in yourself If you lack self-confidence, you can't continue your craziness for too long. It is essential to change your outlook and live an entirely new life, one that anticipates greater things.

Chapter 11: A Philosophy to Increase Your Self Confidence

Everyone is extremely proud of their achievements. Every one of us is an individual star, be it by our previous accomplishments or the current standards of living.

But, a lot of us have probably snubbed this truth. In fact it should come as no surprise that everybody is capable of doing anything if they dedicate their energy and their lives to it. Everyone is able to enjoy the achievements of life. The only people who struggle are the ones who do not enjoy the privileges. Are you one of them?

Then, repeat your reply to yourself. Whatever the outcome make sure you make the situation better.

It's fantastic if you are able to affirm that you're able to have confidence in yourself. But, don't limit yourself to the things that are adequate. There will always be gaps so be looking for ways to grow.

If you said "no," don't worry. If you had devoted your entire life to the irrational shouts of despair, you will surely be remorseful at every decision.

It's a pain knowing that you have everything you needed to be successful and yet you didn't make use of it.

A young eagle lived in a village of chickens and was born there. He was taught that he was an animal which he was then taught to be one. He has been looking at the magnificent eagles flying in the air for a long period of time.

He wished he was born like these eagles flying through the air every when he takes a moment to be in admiration of their majestic flight. Although his heart desires to reach the heights that eagles can reach however, he was hesitant to fly. He didn't realize his full potential or even who he was.

As it turned out, he ended up as a chicken, constantly yearning to be among those whom the real him truly belongs.

All of us belong to the family of eagles. We are all able to fly to the maximum of our capabilities. We'll always be stifled by our inability to climb new levels and become the individuals we were made to be if we do not allow ourselves to fly and find out our true identity.

We could have all lived happy and contentment had we only recognized the eagle who is sleeping inside us.

We all were born with pride and accomplishments. We cannot be grateful to our Universe enough for making the effort to ensure that we have everything that we require to fly. Don't lose this opportunity by carrying things on your back that hinder your from taking off.

Imagine a chicken that is able to emerge from the mud, like an Eagle. Chickens are genetically bred to be killed. Similar to that should we decide to become chickens, we must accept that our purpose could be achieved. In other words, we should praise the universe for having been a good defender and has provided our with all we require.

Take on the role of an eagle, and lead a life that is free of the unhealthy chicken culture. Take on the role of an eagle and make use of the confidence that comes from being a strong creature for your benefit.

Chapter 12: Building Confidence and Self Esteem

Optimism! Everything is determined by what we believe about ourselves as individuals as well as what we observe around us, and even life itself. We're bound to live our life to the extent which every human being should when we believe in the goodness of it.

Unfortunately, many of us struggle to find a reason to feel optimistic in an environment of challenges as well as morbidity and sorrow. It is evident that happiness and pleasure do not have to be incompatible; else life would be empty. If all we can think about is happiness, pain will never be experienced. If we could always be content, our tears would cease to be meaningful. If we didn't stumble every now and then fall, our confidence will not be recognized.

We can design anything we'd like out of our lives that is a wonderful privilege. To make sure we do not miss unforgettable moments that can never happen again We must start the foundational work we'll need to do early. One moment in time is lost for ever, but the light you shine will be a treasure even after you've left.

We'd be able see the fullness of our potentials and be optimistic about the future. Everyone has the chance to be noticed. However, many of us quit before we even begin the fight since we do not want make a statement.

It is essential to be bold in order to be able to be a part of what the world has got to provide. Even the fears of self-confidence and low self-esteem can't hinder you from living your life to its maximum.

The people who are confident in themselves are the ones who have fought through the challenges of. To see what is before us, sometimes we need to risk it all. But, taking risks requires confidence in oneself. It's like being an armed warrior without this.

We were all given the capabilities we'll be able to use in our later years since the moment that we came into the world. One of these abilities is the ability to confront the challenges by faith, not just within ourselves, but also in God, the one who created us all.

Although it may seem like the other person has more luck than we are, we have all were given the same opportunities to grow in the self-esteem we have.

In reality life isn't unfair We are conditioned to believe that it is. Everyone has their fair portion of blessings as in adversity. It all comes down to our perspective of the events and how we handle them.

Confidence and self-esteem are the identical thing. Because he's more articulate and confident than the majority of us, he's more comfortable with his own weight, and better equipped to stand up in front of the crowd and many people think that the person we admire has many of the blessings of life. Remember that before getting there the first time, he faced challenges that helped increase self-confidence and confidence. All of us can become that person with enough self-confidence.

To build solid foundations for confidence and self-esteem the only thing we have to do is discover the inner wisdom within us. Before we are able to accept help from others, we have to originate from within. If you do not wish to accept this basic truth, external reinforcement will not help you understand the value of you and how well you were made.

Take the time to discover who you really are. It'll be one of your most important life choices.

Chapter 13: The Roots of Low Self Confidence

We're unable to pinpoint a single cause to blame for low self-confidence.

In actual fact what we're failing to discover and correct are the results of previous mistakes and mistakes. It's the result of our inability to understand our true identity and the obstacles standing against our personal growth.

Self-confidence is a problem that can be impeded. It will force us to use our strengths and view our mistakes as early defeats. We'd be confined to our comfortable surroundings where everything is shielded from continued mistakes as well as embarrassment. The comfort zones then convince us to not leave its four corners, because there are losses and disappointments to come.

We must be wary of from giving into the critic within us, regardless of how we are told how rough and unorganized things could be. We must at least be able to defeat it and show our superiority to others.

As we grow older, we begin to develop confidence issues in ourselves. Many of us have teachers, parents as well as friends and foes who're more concerned with our shortcomings than with our virtues. They will smother our inner drive and remind us of our mistakes. Although they might not say these things out in public their actions and laughter are enough for us to believe that we're the losers.

There is a chance that you live in the shadows of harsh eyed, critical eyes who don't see the flaws in you. Perhaps you're an underling to a sibling who does well at school, which is the reason for the constant disregard for you and the intense concentration on him. If you feel that you're not able to do things by yourself, you will find that people likely do things for you.

These are the subtle triggers that could eventually cause you to lose faith in yourself.

Soon you'll realize you're not capable of accomplishing things, even though you have talents that go beyond your understanding due to poor role models and a lack of interest.

You could then blame all your failings on you as a result of your beliefs in their convictions. You may even convince yourself that you're the only one to blame for the mistakes of the people you share a close relationship.

You'll be accustomed to make broad statements as you grow older. Without the help of the people who have twisted opinions You will be convinced that you're stupid.

Furthermore, as the process continues you'll gain the ability to disregard the defiant allegations made against you. Additionally, you will learn to accept that there's no greater thing in life other than failures and losses that would add additional miseries to the already overwhelming list of problems.

In this moment your self-esteem has dramatically decreased. This means that you'd be reluctant to attempt to solve the conflict you have over your self-esteem and would not even think of ways to escape the life that afflicts you. However, you'll come across ways to solve the problem and individuals who can help. But, your response will be either to ignore them or even remove them from your life.

If you persist through this stage it will be apparent that you're on your journey to recovering from your low self-esteem, but you're too lost in your personal world that it is difficult to tackle the problem. In the event that a miracle that will transform your life occurs.

Chapter 14: Thoughts on Improving Self Confidence

Do not fall for it. Even the most confident individuals have doubts and even the most skilled people have flaws.

There are times when we have thought about becoming the perfect person that we admire in other people however, we must be aware that there is no perfect way to live. Even if our intentions were considerate, the events we'd like to see take place in our lives won't always go as we would like to. If we don't put in the effort to getting our goals accomplished those things that we desire won't come true. To make things be accomplished takes the effort.

Furthermore, the self-confident people haven't stumbled upon their appearance through accident. Someone wrote once"The most gorgeous people" don't simply happen to be gorgeous. Before they can truly appreciate the extent of their value, they have to first experience suffering, hardship and struggle. and even loss.

Every person is built to achieve the best, fame and recognition. The capacity to feel confident is in each one of us and is not something that happens randomly. As with everything else, we're at the same level as those around us. However, the way we approach it and how we respond to the skills we are given make the distinction.

The context that we grew up in as well as the opportunities that made us into the person who we are now, as well as our reactions to the challenges we faced contribute to the early development of self-confidence.

We all know the feeling of being disregarded or encouraged when you are young. We already know how to understand what is happening to us, even if we are still very young. It is possible that the rest of life be dependent on the events that occurred through these years when we were unable to respond positively in childhood due to reasons like insufficient understanding, inadequate models or inadequate guidance.

But, maturation comes with the passage of time. In addition the experiences we're traversing help us to grow. We are aware that experiences are among the most effective teachers we can have. If we don't make the most of the lessons we learn from then we'll only find ourselves back in the same spot until we determine the reason why we failed. So, there's no reason to think that we weren't given the chance to learn from each event.

The truth is that growing older is all it takes to increase confidence in oneself. It is difficult to realise that you are living more than just mediocre when you are accustomed to the thought of falling behind due to lack of success and recognition.

In spite of how we have been back in the day, any person can build confidence. Present is what matters. It is certain that you will be on the way to self-confidence if examine yourself and believe that you're capable of becoming anything and everything you'd like to be.

There are a variety of actions you can take to improve confidence in yourself. The most important thing is to believe that you are able to be any person and are able to be anything you set the effort into. Positivity that states "anyone can do anything" is equally important.

Think back to the times you felt great because you could achieve something and feel good about yourself, even if nothing else else did. You'll be motivated to be the person that you've always wished to be in this way.

Chapter 15: What to Do When You Need to Boost Your Self Confidence

The most dramatic changes can be caused by minor changes. It all boils down to one idea that can help you feel more confident about yourself.

Do you remember a moment where you were convinced that you'd done the right thing that you heard someone say something negative about it? Do you remember a time when you were told that you would not be promoted and you struggled to complete your work in time?

Do you remember the time you set out for yourself to complete a mile? And people looked suspiciously at you due to it? Be aware of those incidents. They all were founded on pessimistic comments that only served to suppress the optimistic side of you that says "You can."

Positive thinking can be a source of confidence. You can build confidence in yourself that you're capable of doing things. This is done by establishing an optimistic outlook on life . You should also take note of your positive qualities are able to demonstrate while contemplating the importance of the negative qualities that you do not have.

Positive thinking doesn't mean that you are positive about something that can't be achieved. Set goals that are achievable, achievable and that don't limit your abilities is essential for boosting self-confidence and positive thinking.

If we are planning to accomplish something, we usually intend to reach targets that are beyond our capabilities, and underestimate our capabilities. We believe that this will motivate us to do two shifts. But what we do not recognize is that if do not meet our own expectations and the expectations of others who surround us, we'll be disinclined to experiment with new ideas.

It's an ideal idea to set realistic goals for our first attempts , rather than chasing unrealistic, inflated goals which could disappoint us.

Be aware that confidence in yourself is determined by the body's hormone balance. You want to feel confident about yourself. In turn, you can inspire yourself to improve your mood. It is possible to use as your "cheerleaders," for example when you remember clearly of having the ability to accomplish some thing or inspired you to accomplish higher goals. If you don't, try to remember those times you were content with your life. Becoming in charge of your moods and feelings will boost your confidence an entire.

We've all been our most scathing critics at some moment during our lifetime. In addition, unfair criticisms lead us to be more susceptible to negative feelings however, they can also alter our perception of life.

Have you noticed that, even though we're not able to say these things to others We constantly critique ourselves? We're more bitter about ourselves than we think. This is why we feel angry and uncertain of ourselves when we receive every negative response from the person who criticizes us. It's as if we tear up long-standing walls for some unjust comments that we seldom require.

Be wary of making generalizations about yourself as making generalizations about yourself will only serve to diminish your self-esteem. Your self-confidence will improve when you re-create the remarks you've made to yourself.

We are the ones to cause destruction. It is possible that we are affected by the negative outlook of those outside. This is true, however, it would only affect us if we allow access to our own. In the end all that's needed is to reinforce your foundations and to create barriers to block negative effects.

Chapter 16: Advises to Help You in Increasing Self Confidence

The basis of life from which we're created is trust. The difference lies in our perception and understanding of our world that surrounds us.

In essence, certain individuals are more observant than others to see themselves and their abilities.

Everything is dependent on how we view our own self, what we know about the possibilities, as well as how effectively we make use of what we know and experience.

We think that everyone other than us, has self-confidence comparable to having a high income. You must realize that the purpose of life is to be egalitarian. Our expectations of what we have , but do not recognize the other people's possessions that we want cause inequality.

Don't judge yourself harshly. Do not deny yourself delights that life offers. Be truthful with yourself and don't give excuses for gazing at neighbor's fences and not paying attention to the gold mine in your own backyard.

Everybody has a beautiful face that nobody is, not even us, is able to take away. Everyone has the capacity to put our talents to good use or not recognize them. The same goes for the beauty of and wonder. We will soon realize that life has much more to offer than just mediocrity once we realize our potential.

But, we have to recognize that there are handful of areas in which we're restricted. But, our ability to be a leader in other fields compensates for the shortcomings. Finding our the right veins and fortes is what is required.

Our prior experiences may limit our comprehension. However, this doesn't eliminate the possibility that we could broaden our view of ourselves when we move one step towards creating positive perceptions of who we are. Remember that the way we handle situations will determine whether or not we succeed or fail. This doesn't mean that if someone succeeds in achieving greater success the achievement is taken from your own vaults. This is simply a sign that the person was able to recognize his strengths and utilizing the knowledge gained to benefit.

A lot of times you can only increase your confidence in ourselves and increase it by attempting things we initially believed were out of our reach. Sometimes , we aren't aware that even doing the simplest tasks can increase our confidence.

There are a variety of ways by that we can increase our confidence. Your self-esteem will be greatly improved by participating in tasks like writing and public relations in order to increase your communication skills.

A majority of us are afraid of speaking in public. Once we get over the fear of speaking it is likely that we will discover more about our abilities in the near future. Learning to develop your own talents can improve your self-confidence.

If you love mixing poetry and notes or have a natural inclination to engage with music, it is possible to to avoid low self-esteem by turning this interest into activities that can be more beneficial. You could be a poet and develop your creativity or write music, and let others enjoy your work.

It is all you have to do is be willing to willing to explore new opportunities. Remember your own self as the sole thing that can stop your growth and the only thing to stop you from finding satisfaction is you. Choose whether you'll be your most formidable enemy or your most valuable advantage.

Chapter 17: Build Self-confidence from Within

If you want to build self-confidence for those who have for a long time believed that their self-worth is not enough the most crucial question to be asked is how to get there.

It's no surprise that those who feel confident have a better handle on themselves as compared to those with an unreliable sense of "self. "They tend to be the people who succeed, the centre of society, and most prominent people. They express their thoughts in a subtle and lucid manner as they walk in a straight line and make an impact on other people. In essence these are people who take care of themselves and can be easily identified at a distance.

People who are confident and self-assured are often adored by the general public. This could be due to their charm or simply because they're naturally very welcoming.

There are also confident people who quit the room to improve the mood.

The two types of self-assurance are quite different. The first one can be damaging to the credibility of an individual and also enhance his appearance. It's a given that if you're overly confident, you would not like people to think about you as an effective person and start to see them as a nuisance to their everyday life.

Self-confidence is a result of inner confidence. External stimulation may be beneficial however, knowing yourself and using this knowledge to increase confidence is the most important factor.

It is important to recognize how your weaknesses as well as strengths should not be a hindrance for you to increase confidence in yourself. Instead, use the things listed above to develop a character that can help your family and friends achieve success.

"Know yourself!" at Delphi"Know yourself!" is what the Oracle states. While this may be a relic from many thousands of years ago, we can still profit from its wisdom. It is undisputed.

Gain confidence and gain know-how. But, remember that you are your own source of information. Therefore, you should accept that the self-doubt demons remain in your mind until you acknowledge your shortcomings and shortcomings.

But, if you're not able to control your own self having too much information about yourself can be risky. You'll be exposed to the flaws in your character, and as you're not in control, it's possible that your own thoughts and feelings can overwhelm your energy. This issue is closely connected to ruminative thinking, in where you constantly reflect on your failures and failures, regardless of your accomplishments.

If you're trying to build self-confidence but are unable to control your own self-esteem you are at danger of becoming confident and forgetting how crucial it is to maintain confidence in yourself. Overconfidence can be as harmful as not having confidence whatsoever as we've already talked about. It could lead you back to failure , or worse, your end in.

One thing that can be detrimental or beneficial is having a thorough awareness of self-awareness. People tend to realize how amazing their creations are through self-awareness. They are taught to appreciate their talents and abilities that are just like the characteristics of others. It's true that we are all distinct.

Looking at the strengths as well as weaknesses more thoroughly will reveal our distinct features. Our natural talents that boost our confidence in ourselves is a reflection of our individuality. Our abilities that we are able to not to acknowledge or to maximize at will, highlight our individuality.

If you've not been able to look at your own life and realize your true self None of these facts will ever be revealed to you.

Defining Self-Love.

How do you define self-love?

Self-love is a feeling of respect for oneself, which grows through acts that help our mental, spiritual and physical growth.

Self-love is putting a significant importance on your happiness and health.

Self-love means focusing on your needs, and not making sacrifices for the benefit of other people.

The act of accepting yourself in a loving and unconditional manner is referred to as self-love. It is about being attentive to and taking care of your personal needs, as well as allowing you to think without judgment.

It's about seeing yourself as deserving, moral valuable, worthy, and content.

Accepting what you are right now, at this moment is what it means to be able to love yourself. It is about recognizing your emotions for what they are , and placing a high value on your emotional, physical and mental well-being. So, we know that being a lover of yourself motivates you to make the right choices in your daily life.

How To Develop Complete Self-Love.

Self-love can be developed through the following methods.

Don't judge or evaluate yourself against others.

Because we were taught as competitive children, the idea of comparing ourself with other people comes naturally to us. However, it can be detrimental.

You are the only person, therefore there's no point in trying to compare yourself with anyone else. Instead, focus on yourself and the path you're on. You'll feel more free simply from the energy shift.

Do not worry about the opinions of others.

Similar to this do not worry about what others consider or expect from your character in the world. It's a waste of time since you aren't able to satisfy everyone, and it will result in you moving slower towards becoming the most perfect version of yourself.

Don't be afraid to make mistakes.

Nobody is perfect and everyone is prone to making mistakes, as we are taught as kids. As we get older the pressure to be successful grows more intense.

Allow yourself to be flexible! Be a little naive so that you learn and grow. Take pride in your achievements of the past. As you go from the man or woman of yesterday, to the person you are today , and is to come tomorrow, you're always changing and growing.

Don't listen to the voice inside your head which tells you to aim to be perfect. You will make a lot of mistakes! These mistakes can aid you in becoming a better person while the lessons that you gain will be invaluable.

Keep in mind that your worth isn't determined by the appearance of your body.

It is vital! The world is brimming with all kinds of things trying to deflect you from this powerful truth. The feeling of being unworthy can sometimes be confirmed by internalized sexual discrimination. It's not the appearance of your body that is important; it's your personality.

Choose what you're most comfortable to wear. Wear clothes that make you feel relaxed, comfortable and happy, regardless of regardless of whether it's more or less.

Get rid of people who are toxic without hesitation.

It is essential to let go, even although it may not be simple. Certain people aren't willing to take accountability for the energy that they send out in the Universe. It is possible to separate yourself from someone you feel have brought toxic energy into your life, and don't want to take accountability for it. Make this decision without hesitation. Although it may be painful, it's essential and is liberating.

Always be mindful of how to protect your motivation. Eliminating yourself from certain situations or people who are contaminating your self-esteem with negative values and self-worth isn't inappropriate nor wrong.

Think about your fears.

Humans naturally fear as do mistakes. Accept your fears instead of to deny them.

Your mental health could be improved by this exercise.

You will be able to gain perspective and pinpoint issues in your life that been causing you anxiety by examining and questioning your anxieties. The anxiety you experience could be reduced, but not completely, diminished because of.

Be confident in your abilities to make informed choices for yourself.

Although often we know the right thing to do but we often doubt our capabilities and ability to behave ethically. Remember that your feelings are real. It isn't a matter of escaping the reality of your life. Make sure you are your most loyal supporter since you're the only one who really knows you.

Take advantage of every opportunity life gives you, or create your own.

There's never an ideal time to make the next important action in your own life. Even with less than ideal circumstances don't let them hinder your progress towards reaching your goals and dreams. Instead, grab the opportunity as it may not happen ever again.

Prioritizing oneself

Don't be ashamed of doing this. Women are particularly susceptible to getting habitual about prioritizing other people. While there's a need and time to do such behavior, this shouldn't turn into an habit that is detrimental to the mental and emotional health of your family or friends.

Take some time out to unwind. It is possible to put lots of strain on your body if you do not take time to relax and recharge. Find the things that ease your stress and make the time for it, whether that's sleeping in or spending time in the beautiful outdoors.

Feel sorrow and joy as much as you can.

Be completely present and fully, if you'd like. Don't be afraid to express your feelings; accept the joy and sadness. Like the way fear can help you recognize yourself, the joy and pain can also bring you to realize that you're not your emotions.

Do your best to show courage before your peers.

Make a habit of talking to your thoughts. Like a muscle, the ability to speak your mind grows stronger as you utilize it. You can sit down at the table, without asking permission. Engage in dialogue. Introduce your suggestions to the discussion. Equally important to anyone else's voice, it is yours to hear therefore, make yourself heard and be active.

Discover beauty in the simple things.

Everyday try to take note of at the very least one wonderful small detail of your surroundings. Consider it a blessing and keep a record of it. Along with giving an outlook, gratitude is vital in helping you discover happiness.

Take care of yourself.

Don't add your critique to the world's many negative words. Be gentle with yourself and refrain from calling yourself slurs. Respect yourself. You've come a long way and have certainly have come a long way. Remember to be happy frequently, not just for your birthday!

Think about the lengths you've come to and how long you've lasted even if you don't feel incredibly powerful. Here you are right here, in the present and extremely strong.

Be mindful of yourself, too. It could take some time to build self-love. However, it will become embedded into your heart with time.

Sure, you'll have issues, but when you look back at these experiences, you'll discover that they were an opportunity to move forward towards becoming the most perfect version of you. Be constant in all of this.

Unlocking Self-Love

There are steps that must be completed before reaching out to self-love. I like to call it the four stages of self-love.

Firstly, Define Your Struggles & Let Yourself Heal.

Every healing process utilizes your mind's power in order to activate the body's healing capabilities. The body becomes lighter, our brains sharper and our spirits elevated. After experiencing healing it makes us more prepared to help others heal as we're going through the process of healing.

Before you begin this process You must be able to be insecure. Then, list the areas you struggle with on a regular basis in your the course of your life. Be honest and open about yourself and discover what your hurts are.

If you do, then will you be able begin to heal? Let yourself be forgiven for any mistakes and set achievable goals to make your life better. One of the ways to achieve this is the identification of ways you can hinder yourself.

Remember the most recent time that you hurt yourself through self-critical criticism. Note everything that happened. This is known as mind mapping. It can assist you in identifying where the negative thoughts are originate from.

We could speak from areas of light and love more clearly than those of suffering and sorrow.

Through the exercise, self-healing can be performed in many methods, including relaxation through breathing, contemplation with yoga or meditation, and creating pleasant feelings that affect the production of endorphins, or often referred to as 'happy hormones. Additionally, art therapy could be an alternative to.

Secondly, Stand Up to Your Negative Inner Voice.

Make sure you are aware when negative feelings occur. If you are unsure of your inner voice that you are unable to control You seek out the root of the painful thoughts. Discover what you require for these situations. Do you think the negative feelings are a disguise for something you'd like to see to have in your life? Release the beliefs that restrict your self-love.

You might be amazed by the words you use to make yourself feel down. If a friend of yours spoke to you similarly to the way you communicate with yourself, you're likely to not maintain that friendship for many years. Learn to help yourself through the eyes of a trusted friend.

Thirdly, Make Your Self-Love Routine.

Discover effective ways to motivate yourself to improve your performance. Learn how to change your mindset to focus on the things you love and prioritize yourself. Track your progress by writing it down so that you can learn to maintain or even speed up your progress.

One way to help in improving your thinking is to repeat affirmations that are positive about yourself. It might seem strange initially but it's an effective and effective tool when practicing self-love.

Fourthly, Lean on Loved Ones.

When you keep track of your efforts to improve yourself, make connections with those who are there to support your efforts. Involve them in your goals you want to reach. In addition, you will establish an understanding of your surroundings, but you could also inspire others to start self-love. The power of encouragement is immense and can be used in both directions. Self-love is a journey, not a goal!

Find ways to better communicate with your family members. If you're feeling depressed let your feelings be known by speaking your thoughts. Inform people that you'd prefer to be on your own. Sometimes all is needed is a some time to recharge oneself.

Fifthly, relax your fears.

Accept your fears and accept the fact that you have experienced them. Human beings are human, and it's normal to feel uneasy and doubt concerning certain aspects of your life.

In removing the guilt you experience for not being happy with every part of yourself and your life, you can only acknowledge your insecurity and let it go. Insecurity can only turn into an obsession as long as you keep feeding it.

Sixthly, acknowledge that perfection isn't possible and accept your shortcomings

We live in an increasingly visual world and the notion of perfect may seem to be unavoidable. However, perfection is a vague idea and isn't really a thing.

Furthermore, the Hollywood actors who appear on TV and in movies aren't the same as they appear in these shows and films. They're airbrushed heavily, even after having a group of makeup artist, spray tanning experts personal trainers along with personal chefs, working to make them look exactly the way they appear.

Therefore, if those with all the support around the globe with the expectation that they appear perfect require to be airbrushed, then why do we believe the idea of "perfection" is realistic or even possible?

Once you have accepted that you aren't perfect, you can be okay with the imperfections of your "flaws" and perhaps you may even begin to love these flaws and appreciate the ways that they create you as unique and beautiful.

Seventhly, identify what is important for you.

When you stop attaching your self-worth to how you look to others, you give your mind the space to discover those things that are essential to your life. Explore the world, in person or online and find what makes your heart sound happy. They are things that your brain deserves to be focused on.

Eighthly, develop to support the things that are vital to you.

After you've determined what's crucial to you, study the issue and then develop your own ideas. Join a class or join an organization, or create time for "you time" to spend thinking about your ideas.

These activities will feed your spirit, making you truly attractive and will allow you be in love with who you truly are. A person who has soul, passion and the desire to be your very best self. Someone who is totally imperfect, but who is becoming more beautiful every day, in ways that matter to them.

Ninthly, rinse and repeat.

Self-love isn't a destination, but rather a continuous deliberate decision. Always check in with yourself to ensure that old worries or new ones don't turn into obsessions. remind yourself of your weaknesses, look at the things that matter to you and come up with new strategies to keep those things in mind.

It's important to keep in mind that self-love doesn't mean liking all of yourself 100%, and that's not feasible. Self-love means not let those thoughts take over us, and about noticing and then renouncing our negative convictions and instead focusing your energy to factors that help us be more happy more confident, healthier, and content.

In the end, small every day steps will help you get on the correct path of the larger journey. Don't be a slave to pressure and take things at your own pace. Self-love doesn't mean pampering yourself with money, though it's not a bad idea to reward yourself throughout the process.

Self-Love

Why is self-love so important?

Self-love is a way to counter negative self-talk and helps put things into the right perspective. Even if the challenges you face result from mistakes you've made Self-love can help you learn from your mistakes and to continue on. This builds your emotional strength and helps you prepare for future challenges.

Why do you think self-love can be so hard?

Self-love can be difficult to accept because of Negativity Bias and growing as a child with a lack of acceptance and a lot of shame It is possible to hold onto our shortcomings, past mistakes and poor choices. We may minimize the positive things about ourselves and our good strengths. Researchers have discovered that our brains have a negative bias.

How do you get of self-love?

Practice proper self-care. You'll be more in love with yourself when you take attention to your basic requirements. Self-love enthusiasts take care of themselves each day by engaging in healthy choices, including regular exercise, healthy eating adequate sleep, intimate and good social relationships.

The signs that show you are in love with yourself.

The practice of self-love is among the most fundamental abilities that one can develop.

When you're experiencing affection for yourself will people accept you as you truly are. While the signals might be different for every person Here are some tangible signs you're loving yourself.

You should surround yourself with people who are concerned about your well-being, who support you and are committed to what is most beneficial for you. You let the connections that are good to thrive , while removing those that are harmful.

It could be meditating every day and eating a balanced diet, working out regularly or any mentioned above. Making yourself and your health at the top of your list is a sign that you value the person you are.

Although it's impressive what they're doing however, it has nothing to do with be concerned with you and the things you can do. It's all about focusing on you and where you're going to be.

Being yourself is important to you , and you're never shy about what you'd like to have or don't want. Your opinion is important and you don't care by what other people believe.

The negative thoughts in your thoughts that can be demotivating and demeaning have turned into positive affirmations. There is no need to tear yourself apart. You believe you're good enough. Everything will go perfectly.

You're driven to achieve your dreams, because they're an integral aspect of who you are and you've got the confidence and trust to push to the extent you'd like.

You're comfortable spending time with yourself , and you appreciate this time with your loved ones. It is essential to recharge your batteries for everyone but instead of feeling guilty about it, you embrace it as it's necessary.

You're thankful. Being grateful is a regular element of our lives. You recognize that you don't owe anything , and feel blessed to have what you do.

You're thrilled when you see others achieve things because you are aware that you're on the path and will experience another, however most important sort of success. You are completely in love with yourself and you're thrilled to watch others succeed.

It is a fact that amazing things will be coming from you since you are sending good vibes out to the universe and are open to a variety of experiences. If you send good energy out there good things will make their way to you.

Then what happens when I am taught to love myself?

Self-love is a call to attend to your requirements. You'll discover how to be kind to yourself, and by doing so, you'll become the person you wish to become. You'll discover the joy and freedom that comes from being authentic to yourself and gain a better knowledge of who you are.

How can you love someone when you aren't yourself?

Yes, you CAN Love Someone Else, Even If You Don't Love Yourself. There's a mythological falsehood that says you must be a lover of yourself before you can let someone else take you in their arms. In reality, most people develop a love for themselves after having first been loved by somebody. If you've never been part of an adoring family member, it's harder to develop a strong self-esteem.

How does it mean to love yourself?

Self-love means the capacity to avoid falling into a pool of self-resentment or shame even when we do something silly. It's about trying new things and knowing that we might fail, without thinking of ourselves consequently being a failure. Self-confidence is often something we acquire because we need to.

How do I tell if someone isn't loving themselves?

People who aren't happy with themselves don't take care of their personal requirements. They'll delay a trip they've always wanted to take for long. In their hearts, they doubt they are worthy of the dream vacation they've always wanted to go on when everything else is first. They are required to be responsible for their children's education or for their vehicle.

What does what does the Bible say about self-love?

Mark 12:30-31 KJV. You must be devoted to the Lord your God with all of your heart and with all your soul and with all your mental faculties, and with all your strength This is the first requirement. The second one is similar, which is this you must treat your neighbors as yourself. There are no other commands more important than those.

The Bible also tells us to be self-loved.

What is the way God desire us to be a loving, self-sacrificing person?

God Wants You to Love Yourself, Too.

A good spiritual life begins by letting yourself be yourself. This doesn't mean that you are in love with yourself or displaying egoism. God doesn't want us to live our lives weighed down by anger, sadness or anxiety about our self.

Does self-love make you selfish?

Self-love is usually regarded to be one of the most pure and clearest forms of selfishness. It is thought of as synonymous with selfishness. To love oneself is be selfish.

Ways to Embrace Self-Love and Thank Your Body

The act of saying "thank you" to people is something you learn at the very beginning. But how often do you give yourself praise?

Giving "thank you" to your body is among the most important actions you can take especially when you're looking for self-love and wellness. It's not a practice that is easy to achieve as society always pressures us to change our lifestyle to conform to a socially acceptable standard.

Meditation

Meditation is an excellent method of focusing on oneself. If life gets hectic and your thoughts are racing you could always try meditation. It is also available to all because you can practice it from any location. All you have to do is find an appropriate, peaceful spot then close your eyes and then breathe.

If you're not sure how to begin or perhaps you would like guided meditation, I would suggest installing an app. There are a lot of fantastic apps out there! One of my personal favorites is known as Insight Timer. It provides 5- to 60-minute and longer-lasting meditations to assist you in calming and rebalancing. If you commit yourself to relaxing your mind every day, you'll enjoy the benefits of meditation as your health advocate

Mindful movement.

Moving your body with intention is quite different than doing exercises or exercising. It's not about forcing you to perform a task that you do not like.

It's about being aware of the body, and then asking what you require. One of my favorite things for moving my body involves walking out along with my pets. I gaze at the sky and the flowers, the trees and the beauty that is all around me. I am aware and present. I love how my body is feeling.

Find a way to exercise that makes your body and your mind feel great. Perhaps a hike or yoga session is the one your looking for? If you're still not finding your preferred mindful exercise continue searching. The best thing of finding it is the ability to pick what you love!

An excellent read.

When I first started to investigate self-love, I didn't understand what self-love was. I was able to understand how to love another but how do I feel about myself?

The question caused me to think about it for a long time each time I was asked or heard me to myself. Sometimes I would even explode in anger, but then I got up in the morning, and while walking to the gym, I said"to myself "maurison are there no books that can help you out here" and I went into the shop and searched for books. I found "The mastery of love" by Don Miguel Ruiz, I bought it and never regretted buying it.

Finding an article (or book!) that resonates with you is a vital aspect of self-love and wellbeing for your mind. Explore the bookshop. Browse through the self-love section and look at what is most appealing to you.

Be surrounded by joy.

Where do you spend the most times? Do you have a workstation at work? Is it in your vehicle? If you look at the surroundings, do you feel an excitement? If not then the next step is to create an environment you really like.

My top things to be surrounded by include activities (especially playing on the playground) and positive words, pictures of the people I cherish and movies, children, as well as my top books and many more. Self-love is a feeling you experience that you're in a cozy space brimming with things that bring you pleasure. If you are able to smile by simply looking at the world, you're practicing self-love!

Request assistance or help.

Self-love is seeking assistance. When you're experiencing a rough moment, you'll find that the majority of people want to support you. It's not easy to open up and reach out for assistance, but one the best ways to cope with an emotional time is to have the help you require.

It's okay to be uncomfortable. It's important to remember that you shouldn't go through it on your own. The assistance you require is a present that you can give yourself.

Find your blissful place.

Everyone should have a place you can go to and be awe-inspiring. For instance, when I'm in need of a boost or a place to reenergize my energy, I go towards the park, the play house or beach or to the gym. There is something relaxing about sitting at the game or playground house, in a relaxing atmosphere, watching children playing with one another or playing football on my PlayStation 5 and eating ice cream, is what I need.

Take a look at where you would like to go. Are you looking for a walk along the beach? An evening with your acquaintances? An exercise class? A class in art? Self-love is all about filling your cup. When you're full it is easier to help others.

Remain calm. We live in the fast-paced world. Allow yourself to take a step back, take in the momentous moments and be kind to yourself. Here are a few ways to slow down your day-to-day life.

Be mindful of your food. Each time when you dine, make the habit of sitting at a table with no distractions. Take care to chew slowly and really feel what you're eating. This simple method can be an instant change in the way you feel within your body each day.

Breathe. Every day, you should spend few minutes breathing. Inhale 10 times and then check in with your body. Let yourself re-center and refocus prior to moving forward with your daily tasks.

Rest. If you feel your body or body is exhausted You must be able to provide your body with the rest it requires. Sleeping in early and not finishing the meal is okay. Not working out so you're home in time to unwind on the couch is fine. It's okay to relax your body. It's after all, the vessel that carries our lives every day, and it needs your attention and love. Relaxing will allow you to regenerate quicker and make you feel better within your body.

Mirror work.

I'm sure you stare in the mirror often. This could be a difficult experience for many people due to the savage inner conversations you listen to. Beware of their comments. Instead, whenever you look in the mirror, gaze yourself in the eye and tell yourself "I love you." Do it even if it makes you feel silly!

Self-talk has proven to be effective. It is also possible to put up some images on your reflection, with lovely, positive reminders. Each day you wake up with a loving and kind message to your body and yourself will enhance the connection you share with yourself effectively.

Gratitude

The idea of having a daily morning and nightly routine that's devoted to appreciation is a fantastic way to improve your self-love. All you require is a notebook to start.

If you get up each morning, and before going to bed, write down three things about which you're grateful. It's a great way to appreciate your self and the life you live. It's an excellent occasion to express gratitude for your body!

Defining Self-Love.

What is self-love?

Self-love refers to a sense of self-esteem that is cultivated through actions which aid in our mental physical and spiritual growth.

Self-love places an emphasis to your health and happiness.

Self-love refers to being focused on your own needs, and not sacrificing to benefit others.

The acceptance of yourself in a warm and unreserved manner is termed self-love. It is about paying attention to being mindful of and caring for your individual requirements, and being able to think freely and without judgement. It's about being able to see yourself as worthy and worthy of moral value and content.

Accepting the way you feel in the present moment, is what it takes to be capable of loving your self. It is about accepting your feelings as they really are and putting a premium on your physical, mental, and mental health. So, knowing that you are self-love can inspire you to make good decisions in your everyday life.

How To Develop Complete Self-Love.

Self-love is possible to develop by following the methods below.

Do not judge or rate yourself in comparison to others.

Since we were educated as competitive kids and accustomed to the idea of comparing ourselves to others is natural to our minds. However, it can be harmful.

You're the sole person in the world, it's not a good idea to measure yourself against someone other than yourself. Instead, concentrate on you and the direction you're taking. You'll feel more relaxed as a result of the shift in your energy.

Don't worry regarding the views of your fellows.

The same applies to HTML0., do not think about what people think or expect from your persona within the society. It's a wasted time as you're not able satisfy all people, and it could lead to you slowing down toward becoming the best version of you.

Do not be afraid to fail.

Everyone is not perfect, and everyone is at risk of making mistakes, just as we were taught as children. As we grow older, the pressure to achieve increases.

Be adaptable! Be a bit naive in order to improve and learn. Take pride in the accomplishments of the previous. As you change from the man or woman you were yesterday, to the person you are today, and the one who will be tomorrow, you're constantly evolving and growing.

Don't believe the voice in your head telling you to strive to be flawless. You will make many errors! These mistakes can help you to become an improved person, while the lessons you learn are invaluable.

Remember that your worth doesn't depend on your appearance.

It's essential! The world is full of things that are trying to divert away from this empowering truth. The feeling of not being worthy can be manifested by internalized sexual discrimination. It's not the physical appearance of your body that matters, but your character.

Select what you're most comfortable in wearing. Wear clothes that allow you to feel relaxed at ease, relaxed and content the fact that it's more than or less.

Remove toxic people and without hesitation.

It is important to let go, while it's not straightforward. Some people aren't ready to accept responsibility for the energy they release into the Universe. It's possible to break away from someone who has created a toxic environment in your life, but aren't willing to accept responsibility for it. You can make this choice without hesitation. While it can be difficult, it's necessary and liberating.

Be aware of the best way to safeguard you from losing your drive. Eliminating yourself from certain people or situations who are damaging your self-esteem with negative thoughts and self-worth isn't inherently inappropriate nor is it wrong.

Consider the things you fear.

Humans are naturally scared as do errors. Accept your fears rather than denying these fears. Your mental health can be improved with this practice.

You'll be able to improve your perspective and see the things in your life that have cause anxiety by taking a look at and asking questions about your worries. The anxiety you feel could be lessened however, it is not completely reduced due to.

Be sure of your ability to make informed decisions on your own.

While we often think we know what the right thing to do, we frequently beg to differ on our abilities and capabilities to act in a moral manner. Remember that your emotions can be real. It isn't an issue of trying to escape the fact that you are living your life. Make sure you're your most faithful person since you're the sole person who truly knows you.

Make the most of every opportunity that life provides or make the one you want to create.

There's never a perfect time to take an crucial decision in your personal daily life. Even with difficult circumstances, do not let them hinder the way you go towards achieving your goals and aspirations. Instead, take advantage of the chance as it's likely to never happen again.

Self-prioritization

Don't feel ashamed about taking this step. Women are more prone to become addicted to prioritizing their own needs over others. While there's an obligation and a the right time to engage in this behaviour, it shouldn't develop into a routine that's harmful to the emotional and mental health of your family members or your friends.

Spend some time to relax. It is possible to put a lot of strain on your body when you don't make time to recharge and relax. Find the things that relieve tension and schedule time to do it, whether it's sleeping in or taking a walk in the outdoors enjoying the beauty of nature.

Feel joy and sorrow whenever you can.

Be fully present and completely as you would prefer. Don't be shy to speak your thoughts embrace the sadness and joy. Like the way that fear can help you identify yourself, the happiness and sadness can make you recognize that you aren't your emotions.

Try to stand up for yourself in front of your fellow students.

Do a regular habit of talking about your ideas. Much like a muscle the ability to talk to your mind becomes more powerful as you use it. It is possible to sit at the table, and not needing the permission. Engage in conversation. Include your ideas in the conversation. Just like the voice of others it is yours to hear , so ensure that you are heard and remain active.

Explore beauty in the most basic of things.

Everyday , keep track of at minimum one amazing element of your life. Consider it as a blessing and record your gratitude. Along with offering a positive attitude of gratitude, it is essential in helping you to find happiness.

Take your care for yourself.

Don't add your criticism to the many negative phrases that are used in the world. Be kind to yourself and avoid calling yourself self-deprecating slurs. Take care of yourself. You've been through a lot and definitely made progress. Be always happy, not just on your birthday!

Consider the lengths you've gone to and the length of time you've been there even when you're not feeling extremely strong. Here you are at the moment and extremely powerful.

Be aware of your own self Also, be mindful of yourself. It could take a while to establish confidence in yourself. However, it will eventually be in your heart over time.

Sure, you'll encounter difficulties, but when take a look back at these events you'll realize that they provided an opportunity to grow into the best version of yourself. Be constant throughout the process.

Unlocking Self-Love

The steps that need to be taken before making the decision to open yourself up for the self-love that we have always wanted to. I like to refer to it as"the four steps of self-love.

Firstly, Define Your Struggles & Let Yourself Heal.

Every healing process uses the power of your mind to boost your body's healing capacities. The body gets lighter, our brains more sharp and our spirits higher. After experiencing healing, we are equipped to assist others during this process.

Before you start this exercise, you must be be not confident. Then, write down the issues you have difficulty with regularly throughout the course of your existence. Be honest and honest about yourself, and identify what your weaknesses are.

If you are, will you be able to begin to recover? Let yourself accept the forgiveness for your errors and set realistic goals to improve your life. One of the methods to accomplish this is by identifying ways that you could make yourself less effective.

Recall the most recent instance that you injured yourself by self-critical criticism. Take note of what happened. This is also known as mind mapping. It will help you in identifying where negative thoughts come from.

We can speak from the realms of love and light more clearly than from areas of pain and sadness.

Through this exercise self-healing is possible through a variety of methods, such as the practice of breathing, meditation by meditative or yoga and producing pleasant emotions that trigger the production of endorphins. They are also known as happy hormones. Additionally, art therapy may be a viable alternative.

Secondly, Stand Up to Your Negative Inner Voice.

Make sure that you are conscious of negative emotions that occur. If you're not sure of the voice in your head that you can't control, Look for the cause of the negative thoughts. Determine what you need in these instances. Are you thinking that the negative emotions are a cover for something you'd love to be able to see to happen in your world? Get rid of the beliefs that hinder your self-love.

You could be surprised at the phrases you choose to feel depressed. If a person you know spoke to you in a similar way to how you speak to yourself, you're probably not be able to keep the friendship for a long time. Learn to aid yourself with the help of a trustworthy friend.

Thirdly, Make Your Self-Love Routine.

Find effective methods to keep yourself motivated to perform better. Learn how to shift your perspective to concentrate on the things you enjoy and prioritize your own goals. Track your performance by recording it so you can be able to sustain or even increase your speed.

One method to assist in improving your mental outlook involves repeating affirmations that make you feel positively about you. It might appear odd at first, but it's an efficient and efficient tool to practice self-love.

Fourthly, Lean on Loved Ones.

If you track your efforts to make yourself better Make connections with people who support your efforts. Include them in your goals that you wish to achieve. Furthermore you'll gain an understanding of your environment as well as encourage others to begin self-love. The potential of encouragement is huge and can be utilized to both sides. Self-love is an ongoing process and not a destination!

Explore ways that you could connect with family and friends. If you're having a bad day, let your emotions be expressed through about your feelings. Inform people that you'd rather be by yourself. Sometimes all you need is a little moment to recharge.

Fifthly, relax your fears.

Accept your anxieties and accept that you've been through the same. Human beings are human beings, and it's normal for you to feel uncomfortable and be uncertain about certain aspects of your life.

In getting rid of the guilt you feel about not being content with all aspects of your life as well as your daily life need only acknowledge the lack of confidence as well as let it pass. Insecurity can become a nagging obsession for as long as you continue eating it.

Sixthly, recognize that perfection isn't possible , and accept your mistakes

We are living in a more visual world , and the idea of being perfect could appear to be a necessity. However, perfection is an abstract concept and isn't a real thing.

Additionally the Hollywood actors in movies and TV aren't exactly the same actors who are in these shows or movies. They're airbrushed extensively and even have makeup artists as well as spray tanning experts who are personal trainers and personal chefs working to create exactly how the actors appear.

So, if the with the greatest support across the world, with the expectation that they will appear flawless, they need the use of airbrushes, what makes us believe that the concept that they are "perfection" is realistic or even feasible?

After you've accepted that you're not flawless, you can begin to be content with the imperfections that are you "flaws" and perhaps you might even start to appreciate imperfections and appreciate how they can make you as beautiful and unique.

Seventhly, consider the most important things to you.

If you let go of attaching your worth to how you appear at others, you allow your mind the freedom to explore the items that are crucial to your existence. Explore the world around you, either in person or on the internet, and find out what is making your heart sing. They are things that your brain is entitled to be focusing on.

Eighthly, create to provide the features that matter to you.

Once you've identified the things that matter to you, research the subject and develop new ideas. Join a class or join an association, or set aside space to set aside "you time" to spend contemplating your thoughts.

The activities listed above will fuel your soul and make you look stunning and will let you fall at peace with the person you have become. A person with soul, passion and a desire to become the very best version of themselves. Someone who is not perfect however, who is getting more beautiful each day by focusing on the things that matter to them.

Ninthly Rinse and rinse.

Self-love doesn't have a final destination and is a continual conscious choice. Be sure to keep an eye on yourself to ensure that any old anxieties or new ones do not become obsessions. Remind yourself of your shortcomings take a look at the aspects that are important to you, and think of ways to keep them in the back of your mind.

It's crucial to remember that self-love does not mean loving everything about yourself which isn't possible. Self-love means to not allow those thoughts to dominate us, and also about taking note of and then abjuring our beliefs about ourselves and focus your attention on things which help us to be content, confident, happier and more happy.

At the end of the day tiny steps every day can help you to get on the right path for the greater adventure. Don't be an oath-bearer to pressure and work according to your pace. Self-love doesn't necessarily mean spending money on yourself although it's certainly an ideal option to give yourself a treat during the course of your journey.

Self-Love

Why self-love is so crucial?

Self-love can be a method to combat self-talk that is negative and help put things in the proper viewpoint. Even if your challenges stem from mistakes you've made , self-love will help you to overcome your mistakes and move in the right direction. This builds your self-esteem and helps to prepare yourself for the future.

What is the reason you think self-love could be difficult?

Self-love is often difficult to accept due to the Negativity Bias, and also growing as a child , with an absence of acceptance and a lot of guilt. it is also possible hold on to our flaws, mistakes from the past and bad decisions. We may ignore the positive aspects about ourselves and the strengths we have. Researchers have discovered that our brains possess an inclination towards negative things.

How can you be a part from self-love?

Make sure you are taking care of yourself. You'll fall more in love with yourself when you pay note of your essential needs. Self-love-lovers take care of themselves every day by making healthy lifestyles, which include regular exercise, eating well, sufficient sleep, and friendships that are intimate and well-established.

The signs that prove that you love you.

Self-love is one of the most essential capabilities that one can acquire. When you're loving yourself, people be able to accept you for who the person you yourself. While the signs may differ for everyone, here are some concrete signs that you're self-love.

You must be around people who care about your health, who are supportive of your goals and believe in the best your wellbeing. You let those connections that are beneficial flourish, while eliminating those that can be harmful.

It could be meditation each day and maintaining a healthy diet, regularly exercising or any of the above. Making yourself and your health top of your priority list is a sign of how much you appreciate the person you are.

Although it's fascinating but it's nothing to do with being worried about you or the things you can accomplish. It's all about you and where you'll be.

Being who you are is essential to you, and you're always open about what you'd love to be or not desire. Your opinion is vital and you're not concerned about what others think.

Your negative thoughts and thoughts that are motivating and negative have changed to positive affirmations. There's no need to break yourself. You believe that you're good enough. Everything will go as planned.

You're motivated to realize your goals, as they're a part of who you are , and you've gained the confidence and faith to push yourself to the level that you'd prefer.

You're content being with yourself and you enjoy spending time with your family members. It is important to recharge your batteries , for all of us however, instead of being apprehensive about it you take it in as it's a necessity.

You're happy. Being thankful is a normal part to our everyday lives. You realize that you don't have any obligations and you feel blessed that you are blessed with what you have.

You're delighted when you observe others accomplish things, because you know that you're in the right direction and will be experiencing a different but more important, type of achievement. You are absolutely in love with you and you're ecstatic to watch other people succeed.

It is an established fact that incredible things can come from you because you're sending positive vibes out into the universe as well as being open a wide range of possibilities. If you radiate positive energy positive things will find their way to you.

What happens if I learn to be a lover of myself?

Self-love is an invitation to meet your needs. You'll discover ways to treat yourself with kindness and, in doing so you'll be the person you want to be. You'll discover the happiness and joy which comes from being genuine to yourself, and gain greater understanding of who you truly are.

How do you love someone if you're not yourself?

You can love Someone else, even if You're Not Loved by Yourself. It's an untrue lie that claims you have to be a self-loving person before letting another person take you into the arms of their partner. However, the majority of people find a deep love for themselves once they've experienced the love of someone. In the absence of having had the privilege of being an affectionate family member it's difficult to establish an esteem for yourself that is strong.

What do you define love for yourself?

Self-love is the ability to stay out of self-resentment and shame, even when we make a mistake. It's about exploring new ideas and being aware that we could fail and not thinking about ourselves being an failure. Self-confidence is usually something we gain due to the fact that we have to.

What can I tell if someone's not enjoying themselves?

People who aren't content with themselves won't manage their own needs. They'll delay an adventure they've always dreamed of taking for a long time. In their minds, they aren't sure if that they're capable of taking the dream trip they've always dreamed of going on, when all else comes foremost. They are obliged to pay for the education of their children or their car.

What does is the Bible tell us regarding self-love?

Mark 12:30-31 KJV. You are to be committed to your Lord God with all your heart, and with all your being and the fullest capacity of your brain and with all your might. This is the primary requirement. The second requirement is the same, that is to treat your neighbors like you. There is no other rules that are more important than these.

It is the Bible also instructs us to love ourselves.

Which is the best way to live? God would like for us to live as a compassionate self-sacrificing and self-sacrificing individual?

God Wants You to Love Yourself, Too.

A healthy spiritual life starts by allowing yourself to be who you are. This doesn't mean you're self-centered or showing egoism. God doesn't wish for us to be filled with feelings of sadness, anger or worry about who we are.

Does self-love make you selfish?

Self-love is generally thought as one of the purest and obvious types that selfishness can take on. It is often regarded as a synonym for self-centeredness. To love oneself is selfish.

Ways to Embrace Self-Love and Thank Your Body

"Saying "thank you" to people is something you learn from the the beginning. But how often do you offer self-praising?

The act of saying "thank you" to your body is one of the most vital actions you can perform, particularly in the quest for self-love and health. It's not an easy thing to master because society constantly insists on changing our lives to conform to the socially acceptable standards.

Meditation

Meditation is an effective technique for focusing on yourself. If life is hectic and your thoughts are racing, you can consider the practice of meditation. It is also accessible to everyone since you can do at any time and from anywhere. All you must do is find the right, tranquil spot and close your eyes then take a deep breath.

If you're not sure where to start or if you are looking for guided meditation, I'd recommend downloading apps. There are lots of amazing apps available one of my favorites is called Insight Timer. It provides five to 60 minutes of longer-lasting meditations that aid you in relaxing and getting your body and mind in balance. If you dedicate yourself to taking time to relax your mind every day, you'll reap all the advantages of meditation. a health advocate.

Mindful movement.

Move your body using intention completely different from doing exercises or working out. It's not about making you perform something you are not a fan of.

The key is to be aware your body and asking for what you want. A few of my most favorite activities to move my body is to walk out together with my pet. I look at the sky, the trees, the flowers and the beauty everywhere. I am conscious and in the moment. I am amazed by how my body feels.

Find an exercise in a way that helps your body and mind feel relaxed and rejuvenated. Perhaps a exercise or yoga class is what you're seeking? If you're yet to find your favorite meditation, continue to search. The best aspect of discovering it is the capability to choose the one you like best!

An excellent read.

At the time I began to research self-love, i did not understand what self-love meant. I was in a position to comprehend the concept of love, but what do I think regarding myself?

The question made me reflect on it for quite a while every time I was asked , or thought of myself. Sometimes, I would get angry however, I woke to work in the early morning and on my way to the gym I said"to myself "maurison do you have any books to help me to get through this" and then I went to the bookstore and began searching for books. I came across "The mastery of love" by Don Miguel Ruiz, I bought it and haven't regretted purchasing the book.

The ability to find an article (or book!) that you can relate to is essential to self-love and a healthy mind. Visit the bookshop. Look through the section of self-love and take a examine what's interesting to you.

Enjoy the joy of being around.

What is the place you spend your most time? Do have a desk at work? Or is it in your car? When you glance around do you feel an sense of excitement? If not, your next task is make an environment that you truly enjoy.

My most loved things to be surrounded by are activities (especially playing in the play area) and positive phrases images of the people I love, movies of children, and my top books, and much other. Self-love is the feeling that you get when you're in a warm and cozy place full of things that bring satisfaction. If you find yourself smiling by just looking around and smile, then you're doing self-love!

Request assistance or help.

Self-love is the act of seeking help. When you're struggling it's likely that most people are willing to help your needs. It's not easy to be open and seek help However, one of the best strategies to handle difficult times is to get the support that you need.

It's fine to be uneasy. It's important to keep in mind that you shouldn't have to go through it by yourself. The assistance you need is a gift to yourself.

Find your blissful place.